OVERCOMING THE LITTLE FOXES

A Blueprint for Outsmarting Life's Challenges

Niyi Borire

OVERCOMING THE LITTLE FOXES: A Blueprint for Outsmarting Life's Challenges

Copyright © Changemakers International 2023

All rights reserved.

No part of this publication may be reproduced, distributed, or transmitted in any form or by any means, including photocopying, recording, or any other electronic or mechanical method, without the prior written permission of the author, except in the case of brief quotations embodied in critical reviews and certain other non-commercial uses permitted by copyright law.

DEDICATION

∴

To everyone who is fed up with an average, middling, mediocre life.

To everyone who desires to live the overcoming life that God has ordained for them.

ACKNOWLEDGMENTS

∙ ∙

I couldn't have pulled off the writing of this book without the inspiration and direction of the Holy Spirit. Lord, I am grateful for the ability to capture and articulate your thoughts.

To my dearest friend and companion – Olayemi – thank you for your constant love and support. I am grateful to God for giving me a wife as caring and understanding as you. Thank you for all that you do to see me become all that God has designed me to be and do all that He has assigned me to do. This book is another testament to that.

Thank you, Omolade Olufowomu, for contributing your story and depth of wisdom to this book. I have no doubts that it will greatly bless the readers.

Finally, I appreciate everyone who has worked hard to make this book project a success. I am deeply grateful for your contributions. God bless you greatly.

A NOTE ON VICTORY: LITTLE THINGS THAT COUNT

••

Many of us think victory is one remarkable thing that would happen in our life. If you ask the average person to tell you about victory, they will think of something grand and spectacular happening to them. Just imagine a madman walking towards you and throwing a bag at you. Then, you open the bag and find a million dollars. That'll be truly incredible!

When we think about victory, we think of the spectacular; we imagine if God is going to give us victory, it will be in a stunning and unusual way, it's going to happen with a big bang. However, your victory will most likely come from little wins. Your victory is going to come from an aggregation of marginal gains. Many times, the successes that we get in life, the victory that God has shown us, is a victory that comes from little things. People who do remarkable things don't just jump out from nowhere; they have been grafting and working hard for a while. Great victories don't just jump out of the sky; they require a little effort here and there. It's the aggregation of small gains that leads to great victories. Unfortunately, we usually don't see those small gains.

Jesus only spent 33 years on earth, and no one knew anything about him for the first three decades. For 30 years, He was anonymous; he was just the son of a carpenter that no one reckoned with. But within three and half years, He changed the whole course of humanity. Some of us are not ready to pay the price of small beginnings and the little efforts needed when we are not known or famous. I am here to tell you that little things count.

What we call little is the foundation of great. The foundation of great victories is the little things. A little egg and a sperm come together to form an embryo, and that little embryo is what forms a whole baby. One single black dot may be the beginning of cancer. Cancer doesn't just explode and become terminal; it starts from a little cell. One little idea may be the beginning of a scientific breakthrough or a revolution.

On a fateful day, the 11th of September 2001, the CEO of a company on the Twin Towers survived because his son started a new kindergarten school. His son started school that day, and he grudgingly went to pick up his son; that was how he missed the incident.

Another guy is alive because it was his turn to bring doughnuts to the office, so he stepped out, and before he came back, the first plane crash into the building had taken place. A woman was late to work because her alarm clock did not wake her that morning. I am sure she was rushing, and by the time she got to the office, something terrible had happened. She would have been very thankful to God for the alarm not working. One of the people who survived missed his bus that morning, and another person spilled food on her clothes, so she had to take time off to change. It was during that period that the crash happened. Another person said his car would not start that morning, while another couldn't find a cab. Another guy put on a new pair of shoes but developed a blister on his foot while he walked to work, so he stopped to buy a Band-Aid, and that is why he is alive today.

How do you react when you are stuck in traffic? How do you react when you miss an elevator or the bus? How do you react when you are in a hurry, and the red traffic light stops you? All these people went through little things that morning, but those little things kept them alive.

Little Sins, Great Condemnation

Catch for us the foxes, the little foxes that ruin the vineyards, our vineyards that are in bloom. (Songs of Solomon 2:15 NIV)

Many great men of God have been brought down by little sins. Little sins can have great condemnation. You look at the life of Samson in Judges 13, 14, and 15, and in every chapter, Samson sees a woman. He was always lusting and seeing women until he fell into the lap of Delilah. Delilah did not happen to Samson overnight. People don't backslide overnight; it's always a little sin, a little compromise, a little lie. Little sins will often have great condemnations. If you allow little sins in your life, cheating on your taxes, cheating on your immigration form, or claiming things you shouldn't claim, God cannot rely on you for the great victories He wants to wrought for this generation.

I know you speak in tongues; I know you lead the choir; I know you can call down fire in prayer meetings; I know you have the titles, but you know that your hands are full of sin. You know there is fornication under your skirts; you know all those things. Little sins can have significant consequences. A little leak from where water enters a ship can sink a great ship. You can't afford to allow little compromises.

How do the Eskimos in Alaska catch wolves for their coats? A single pack of wolves can run for 20 kilometres without stopping. Wolves are tough to catch. Eskimos don't just go around chasing wolves; they catch wolves by killing a deer and freezing the blood in the snow. They get a double-edged knife so sharp it can slice anything. They hide it there so that the wolf smells the blood of the deer from kilometres away. When it gets to the blood, it starts licking it like a lollipop. Just imagine licking a lollipop with a sharp knife, and soon it slices the tongue of the wolf. That wolf will not die in one hour or two hours; the Eskimos will wait for hours, even days. A little bleeding at a time, and the wolf will bleed to death. Then the Eskimos take the wolf.

Some of you are licking the lollipop of sin and compromise, not knowing there is a sharp knife underneath. It might just be tapping the bum of your co-worker as a married man or watching pornography. God can't go far with you. That's why today, you are going to make up your mind that you will not allow a little sin to rob you of the victory God has for you. God wants to do something special in your life, but a little sin will not allow Him to do that. I know you are not a terrorist; you will not take the gun to a shopping centre to shoot people; I know that you are not a denier of God; I know you are not an atheist, but why are you allowing little compromises here and there?

Today, God is calling you to a higher level, a higher life. A little sting by a bee can paralyse a man. I know a man who had Tick Paralysis; a little tick can bite a person and paralyse the person. It's like giving someone a shot of Botox; it paralyses the entire muscles of the body. A little stone in your kidney can give you great pain. A little injury can bring the most talented athlete down. You are useless if you carry a spiritual wound, no matter how anointed you are. A wounded soldier is a nuisance. If Lionel Messi or Cristiano Ronaldo has a little groin strain, they are useless in a game. A little sin can drain all the anointing upon your life.

'Wherefore seeing we also are compassed about with so great a cloud of witnesses, let us lay aside every weight, and the sin which doth so easily beset us, and let us run with patience the race that is set before us, (Hebrews 12:1 KJV)

Sin is like a small pebble in a shoe. Have you tried walking with a small pebble in your shoes before? It's so uncomfortable. Some people are running in life with pebbles in their shoes. Those little injuries can lead to significant complications. Yes, I know you have not been knocked out yet. Yes, I know you still come to Church to pray, but you have been wounded. Little struggles lead to great weariness, little setbacks lead to great collapse.

There is a way out - Don't ignore the warnings. Instead, deal with sin; a little smoke can lead to a great fire.

Abstain from all appearance of evil. (1 Thessalonians 5:22 KJV)

Flee also youthful lusts: but follow righteousness, faith, charity, peace, with them that call on the Lord out of a pure heart. (2 Timothy 2:22 KJV)

If you give the devil an inch, he will take a mile. So if you don't want to eat the devil's apple, don't go into his garden.

Little Stains, Great Consequences
Some blemishes in our lives are not sins, but they will still limit us. Imagine yourself as a bride wearing your dress on your wedding day and there is a stain on it. Would you go out with a stain on your wedding dress? No! You will make sure it is clean. They would have to find a way to delay the ceremony. Everyone will have to wait because you will not walk to the altar with a stain on your wedding dress. In the same way, we have got to deal with those stains in our lives because they can have tremendous consequences.

Six Stains You Have to Deal With
1. Regret over yesterday's failure
Forget the past and move on. I know you have made mistakes; we all do; we are all flawed, and we are blessed with imperfections. However, you cannot live in the past; you have got to forget the past and move on. Don't be like that drunken man who was paddling all night expecting to cross the river to the other side only for the next day to come, and he was still at the same spot because he had forgotten to untie his boat. Now is the time to move on without any regrets. All things work together for your good, including your mistakes.

2. Anxiety over today's problems

Little stress will lead to a great depression. So don't let anxiety stress you, don't let anxiety weigh you down. You cannot solve every problem.

3. Worry over tomorrow's uncertainty

Worry does not empty tomorrow of its sorrow; it empties today of its strength. Worrying is like racing the engine of an automobile without letting go of the clutch. Worry is like a rocking chair; it keeps you busy but doesn't take you anywhere. The more you pray, the less you panic. The more you worship, the less you worry. When you are worried, worship.

4. Procrastination over present duty

A little sleep, a little slumber, a little folding of the hands to rest— and poverty will come on you like a thief and scarcity like an armed man. (Proverbs 6:10-11 NIV)

Little sleep – Great Poverty. Don't postpone it when the Lord gives you prompting.

5. Resentment of another's success.

Resentment is a mixture of anger, disappointment, and fear. Eleanor Roosevelt said, 'No one can make you feel inferior without your permission'. It does not mean you are perfect; it just means that the feeling of inferiority is something you allow to happen.

6. Unbelief in God's providence
Your situations sometimes will make you doubt God's providence, but you have to trust God's plans and purpose for your life. He has got you covered.

Little Strength, Great Conquest
I know thy works: behold, I have set before thee an open door, and no man can shut it: for thou hast a little strength, and hast kept my word, and hast not denied my name.
(Revelation 3:8 KJV)

Great victories are for people with little strength. Great victories are not for the Captains America and Australia. Great victories are for those with little strength and great faith.

- **Little Stature, Great Legacy** – Mother Teresa was not tall, but she left a legacy of love and compassion on earth. You might be small in stature, but God is planning a great legacy for you. It is not the size that matters; it's the content.

A whale was swimming in the ocean and right in the centre of the ocean was this small, plastic container cork, it was right there on the sea. The whale said, 'Move away,' but the cork said, 'No! I am resting and this is my spot'. The whale said, 'If you don't move away, I will strike you and you will disappear'. The cork said, 'Go round past me, you met me here and I am not moving'. The whale picked the cork with its tail, threw it into the sky, and disappeared into the clouds. The whale smiled and said, 'I warned you'. But the cork landed on the same spot; gravity brought it back there. The whale said, 'I will teach you a lesson', then it hit the cork down, and it went down into the sea, and the whale thought it got rid of the cork, but the cork floated back to the same position. The whale hit it again but it popped up once more and the cork said, 'I am made of stuff that cannot sink. I might be small in stature, but I am unsinkable'.

Who is there with little strength but great faith? Your start might be small, don't despise those things you can do well. It takes tiny miracles to amaze you and change your world. Little steps in the right direction can lead to outstanding achievements. Take that step today; stop waiting for you to show up on CNN, and stop waiting for a big break, instead take a little step. Little steps lead to great achievements. A little seed can lead to a great harvest; just plant that little seed. Use what God has given you. Use what you have, don't complain about what you don't have. Don't complain about the size of your seed because in your seed are fruits, in those fruits are seeds, and in those seeds are trees. Don't despise your seeds.

Little Savings, Great Profits
Be grateful for your little successes; they aggregate as great victories. Improve your performance in little ways.

Exodus 23:30 KJV says, *'By little and little I will drive them out from before thee, until thou be increased, and inherit the land'*.

God did not wipe the Canaanites out of Canaan all at once, He did it little by little. Sometimes, the great victories we want will be an aggregation of marginal gains. Little service, great exploits.

'He that is faithful in that which is least is faithful also in much: and he that is unjust in the least is unjust also in much' (Luke 16:10 KJV).

Show me a man or woman who cannot bother to do the little things, and I will show you a man or woman who cannot be trusted with great things. Never neglect the little things. Don't ignore those little things. You may not have much; give the little you have all the same. Little obedience attracts great blessings.

CONTENTS

∙∙

DEDICATION	iii
ACKNOWLEDGMENTS	iv
A NOTE ON VICTORY	v
INTRODUCTION	xix
Chapter 1: GUILT AND REGRET	1
Chapter 2: REJECTION	13
Chapter 3: FEAR AND ANXIETY	39
Chapter 4: LONELINESS	51
Chapter 5: PROCRASTINATION	63
Chapter 6: EMOTIONAL PAIN	71
Chapter 7: DEBT	81
Chapter 8: NEGATIVE MINDSETS	91
Chapter 9: BUILDING HEALTHY RELATIONSHIPS	115
Chapter 10: EXCEEDING EXPECTATIONS	135

INTRODUCTION

••

It was Roger Crawford who said, *'Being challenged in life is inevitable; being defeated is optional'* In other words, challenges are as normal as life itself. And while some people may feel more disadvantaged than others that they term 'privileged', everyone on earth has their fair share of challenges. They come in different forms, in different ways, and at different levels, but they are common to all. So, no one is exempt from the claws of life's challenges. In the final analysis, therefore, every man has a responsibility toward their challenges – to overcome or accept defeat.

Yes, the struggles of life are real, and the limitations and difficulties we encounter can be overwhelming. However, God's intention for His children is to overcome regardless of what comes up against them. Jesus assured us in His Word, *'I have told you these things, so that in me you may have peace. In this world, you will have trouble. But take heart! I have overcome the world'* (John 16:33 NIV). Jesus prepared our hearts for these struggles, challenges, or limitations. We may not be able to avoid them, but we have all it takes to overcome them – He already overcame them on our behalf! And that's good news! Because He overcame, we can always overcome too. We must settle this in our minds. It can make all the difference. It helps us fight with the right mindset – that victory is already ours before any battle. We are overcomers!

In this book, I have analysed a few areas of challenges or difficulties that are common to us all and then present pragmatic insights and measures that can help us overcome in those areas. I have approached these topics from a universal, personal, and professional point of view to ensure that this book can become a life manual for you, my dear reader, guiding you into a life of perpetual victory.

As you read through the following pages, let me tell you upfront that overcoming should not be optional for you in any facet of your life – it is your right to overcome. In fact, you were designed to overcome. The winning DNA is in you. You have got what it takes to keep winning. But you must first believe this before it can be your everyday reality. You must make up your mind that you will never allow life's challenges to throw your back on the ground. It is not normal to get floored by the things you were created to trump. And just in case that has been your story, then I am glad that you have before you right now a manual that will help you switch lanes. It is time for you to return to the overcoming side where you belong.

I trust God that this book will help you retrace your steps and retake your life. It is my prayer that as you read this book, your hope will be restored, and faith will rise in your heart to continually live the life God intended for you – an overcoming life!

1
GUILT AND REGRET

≈≈≈

IT WAS 9 PM ON a dry Sunday evening on the 8th of October 1871 when the great Chicago fire occurred. Interestingly, the great American Evangelist, DL Moody, was holding his Sunday evening service at the time the fire began. He was about to round off the service when the sound of fire trucks and church bells enveloped the area. In his mind, he thought it would be nice to give the congregation some time to think about their salvation so they can make a lasting decision, rather than make the usual salvation call immediately, he decided to delay it till the following week, hoping that they will all return to make a decision for Jesus. His intent was that they should accept Jesus into their lives because of who He really is not because of the pressure the preaching moment may have brought.

Unfortunately, this was not to be because that night, the raging inferno destroyed more than 9sqkm of the city, including over 17, 000 structures which left more than 100, 000 residents homeless and stuck. Moody's church was not spared either. In fact, after the fire, Moody said, *'All I had left was my family and my Bible'*. This incident shook DL Moody to the core. He was never the same again. He became ill because of the guilt he carried. Being a passionate evangelist and soul winner, he grieved when he missed the opportunity for people to come to the saving knowledge of Christ.

In his own words, he said, *'I have never dared to give an audience a week to think about their salvation. If they were lost, they may rise in judgment against me. I have never seen that complication since and I will never meet those people until I meet them in another world. But I want to tell you of one lesson that I learnt that night, which I have never forgotten, and that is, when I preach, to press Christ upon the people there and then and try to bring them to the decision on the spot. I will rather have my right hand cut off than give an audience a week now to decide what to do with Jesus'*. (Sources: Harvey, Bonnie C. 1997. DL Moody: The American Evangelist. Ohio, USA. Balbour Publishing.)

The story of DL Moody is a very powerful illustration of guilt and regret. Guilt and regret are both universal emotional expressions that we experience at different times in our lives. The main issue is not about experiencing any of these emotions but about how we deal with them. Guilt is the feeling you have when you have done something morally or ethically wrong. On the other hand, regret is the emotion that arises when an individual believes that their past action or behaviour, if changed, might have achieved a different outcome. If you do something that you feel by moral, ethical, or religious standards is wrong, you feel guilty. You feel guilt when your actions or inactions are wrong. Sometimes, we feel guilty when we are caught doing something wrong, but we don't feel regret about it. A lot of criminals, for example, especially psychopaths feel that way. Usually, they will plead guilty to a crime but what they are actually saying is, *'Yes! I know I'm guilty, I broke the law but if I wasn't caught, I will do it again and again'*.

Regret often happens when you realise that you should have done something in a better way than it was actually done. So, regret arises from having a better understanding of the situation. Most times, when we make decisions that may not be morally or ethically wrong, we have feelings of regret around the situation because we feel that we didn't know enough or better. Regret often comes through reflection. Regret often shines the light on our humanity – that we know in part and that our decisions (which may not be morally or ethically wrong) can lead to consequences that are unfavourable. These unfavourable results may create feelings of regret.

Sometimes, people also feel regret over things they have no control over. Even in situations where an alternative behaviour or decision was impossible, people still find creative ways of blaming themselves for things outside of their control. The basis for this is a lack of compassion for self or self-worth. Some people blame themselves or have regrets over the choices of others. For example, many mothers of criminals repeatedly blame themselves for not doing enough because their sons or daughters made the wrong choices. The same is also true of spouses who have regrets over the bad decisions made by their spouses, which can then result in harm to others.

Regrets can come from our pride or ignorance. Mr O. Henry writes about the kind of guilt or regret that can cripple someone when it comes from one's pride or arrogance:

'Just back from attending the wedding of his beloved with another man, Trysdal is sharing a drink with his friend, the bride's brother who has arrived from South America, pondering over, and why he lost the bride to another man. They had never really fought before they drifted apart. One particular romantic evening, basking in his beloved's admiration, Trysdal allowed her to believe that he spoke excellent Spanish (which is not true). This was also the evening he asked her to marry him. She promised to respond in a day. The next morning, Trysdal received from her a cactus in a red earthen jar with a foreign-sounding name tag. Receiving no other message and too proud and vain to seek her out, Trysdal took this as a refusal. They met a few days later. She looked at him hopefully and getting no response, 'turned to snow and ice'. This was how they split up.

Now in the present, the bride's brother points to the cactus and asked Trysdal where he got it from. Immersed in his regretful thoughts, Trysdal says, a friend gifted it to him. So, the brother then delivers the bell! He mentions casually that this cactus was common in South America and the Spanish name on the tag, Ventomarme, which in English means, 'Come and take me.'

Trysdal was plunged into depths of regret and sorrow following this revelation. Proud and egotistical, he had managed to ruin his life because he couldn't bend enough to ask his beloved why she had not responded to him. And of course, it was vanity that led him not to tell her that he didn't know any Spanish. With that one white lie, he buried his future with her.

Both guilt and regret can co-exist but oftentimes, they can occur on their own. Regret, in particular, can be quite painful. You can marry a tongue-speaking, Bible-quoting person and both of you may not be compatible in any way. Marrying that person is not morally wrong but you may regret the decision due to a lack of compatibility or commonality. This can be quite painful. However, sometimes, a feeling of regret may be because you have not seen the bigger picture. Many times, we have regrets over our decisions because of the temporary pain and suffering we go through without realising the bigger picture.

A case study is Joseph who had shared his dreams with his brothers, however ill-advised that was, it was important that his family members hear about his dream. Unfortunately, that created resentment and anger in his brothers which resulted in them trying to kill him, if not for Reuben's intervention. He was later sold to slavery just because of his dreams and his position in the family as the favoured son. He could have regretted the path he was taking. I believe he would have had feelings of being ordinary and probably preferred not to have a dream at all.

However, if he had seen the bigger picture, he would have known that God had a plan in mind for him. The emotions of regret can come when we go through temporary or transient pain in our journey to our glorious destiny. The scripture says *that our light affliction worketh for us a greater glory* (2 Corinthians 4:17 KJV). It is indeed true that whilst we are going through a light affliction, we may have regrets about the choices we have made to pursue our destiny. However, we should be encouraged because if we are on the right path, we will undoubtedly enjoy the reward, in Jesus' name.

Guilt can also paralyse a person and make them feel very useless. It can lead to depression, anxiety, and impair one's performance. I once read the story of Katherine Ann Pal, who was an American ex-convict and long-term fugitive along with her accomplice Susan Saxe, who was placed on the FBI's Most Wanted list in the '70s after the two of them had participated in robberies at several banks – one of which led to the death of a Boston police officer. Katherine remained at large for 23 years. However, in September 1993, she gave herself up. She was in a getaway car for the robbery when the Boston police officer was shot but she had not shot the man.

In court, she said, '*His death was shocking to me. I have had to examine my conscience and accept any responsibility I have for the event that led to it*'.

Katherine was sentenced to 8-10 years in prison for the bank robbery. You wonder why she voluntarily surrendered to the authorities when they might never find out. Well, I am sure she just couldn't live with the guilt anymore. Guilt can drain away happiness, confidence, and pleasure. It can make a highly functioning person operate at a low level without being able to achieve what they intend to. It can also foster other negative emotions that can lead to depression and even suicidality in some other instances.

Although guilt and regret are universal emotions and part of our human experience, we can take steps that will manage them effectively so that they don't ruin us. It's good for us to take responsibility for what we have done wrong, but we must strive to balance out these feelings so that they don't take away our future happiness and motivation. This is because guilt and regret can cause deep psychological issues and cripple you if you don't address or deal with them immediately. You can't change the past, but you can certainly recreate your future. I have listed a few tips below that will help you manage guilt and regret:

1. **Acknowledge your wrong and take responsibility for your actions**: It's important to understand what you have done and openly acknowledge it. You should also take responsibility for your actions and make necessary restitutions if required. If it is very difficult to publicly acknowledge that you have done something wrong, then you should seek counsel from your spiritual leaders, coaches, or mentors so you can be guided.
2. **Take time to reflect**: Having a deep reflection or review of the situation will give you a better understanding of what you have done wrong and why you did it. It may also help you see what you could have done differently and how to alter the outcome in the future. The greatest regret you may have is not stumbling on a stone but stumbling on it again in the future. By evaluating your decisions, you know how to avoid the situation in the future. Don't just spend time replaying your mistakes from the past but reappraising the situation for what you can do better next time.
3. **Focus on the things you can change and let go of the things you cannot change**: You must learn to carry your burdens. We are humans and our capacities are limited – we can't change

everyone, not even Jesus reached or saved everyone. You must stop fretting over situations beyond your control or over other people's actions that you can't help. Don't get stuck in the vicious cycle of self-regret.

4. **Forgive yourself**: Give yourself enough time to replenish and heal. If you have done something wrong, you must be ready to let go of the feelings, whether it is a lost relationship, collapsed business, or poor health. The past is gone, and being stuck on the rollercoaster of stress and worry will keep you busy but take you nowhere. You must also learn to practice self-compassion. Self-compassion promotes self-forgiveness. If you will not make those exact choices in similar situations today, you are incriminating yourself as an innocent person. So, learn to forgive yourself.

5. **Seek forgiveness from anyone involved and seek reparations if possible**: It's not enough for you to seek forgiveness from God for your actions. You should also reach out to those that were hurt by your actions. Remember to seek counsel, if necessary, as stated earlier. Nothing is better than having inner peace.

6. **You should make a plan to change**: Someone said if you fail to plan, you are planning to fail.

This is important for behaviours that are repetitive. If you find yourself repeating the same mistakes, especially if you are susceptible to addictive behaviours, you must be intentional about changing. You may need an accountability partner, learn a new skill, join a self-development programme, have special prayer or deliverance sessions with your pastor, etc. You must be intentional about changing.

7. **Seek professional help**: Sometimes, you need someone to hold your hands through. If you are having feelings of anxiety and depression which would be addressed in subsequent chapters of the book, you should seek help. By seeking psychological or spiritual help, you will be able to manage self-destructive thoughts and emotions by redirecting any negative impulses into more constructive ways of thinking.

8. **Practice gratitude**: There is always something to be grateful for. If you regret losing a close relative, you should be grateful that you have not lost everything. You may regret failing an exam but you should be grateful that you have not failed in life. There is always something to be grateful for or be grateful for. God has blessed us in so many ways that should provoke gratitude but guilt and regret prevent us from

being grateful to God for those blessings. Gratitude is important in handling self-defeating thoughts and forming healthy behaviours that will help us improve our lives so that we can become all that God has designed us to be.

'Only when you let go of your guilt will you be able to move on with your healing process'. Jacqueline Sewell

2
REJECTION

≈≈≈

By Omolade Olufowomu

I REMEMBER THAT I had paid my tuition fees. I was excited about studying Law and was already in the final registration phase when they said they had changed the rules. The admission requirements for the Law degree did not include credit or distinction in mathematics. What was required was an ordinary pass until the University Council changed the rules in the middle of the game. To study Law, they would no longer accept a pass in Mathematics; the minimum grade required was credit.

Well, it happened that Maths and I were not friends. If I struggled with any subject, it was Mathematics. In every high school subject, I had distinction or credit - except for Mathematics where I got a pass. The university refused to enrol me and refunded my tuition fees. I had to move back home; the shame was unbearable. The rejection made me feel like the earth should open up and swallow me. I wished I could rewind time and rewrite history. But, instead, I snuck back home at night because of the shame. I could not stand meeting the same people I had said goodbye to a few days earlier.

I felt rejected. It remains one of the biggest rejections I have ever suffered to date. I was already accepted, I had already gotten everything I needed, and then rejection came up. The next day, my mum said we should go out together but I told her I was not going anywhere. I didn't want anyone to know that I was in that compound.

Rejection actually comes with a feeling of inadequacy. Rejection comes with a feeling of *'I am not good enough'*. Rejection makes you feel undeserving and unwanted. As human beings, we personalise rejection. I didn't consider that the school rules had changed (which wasn't my fault); I thought it was all about me. I wasn't good enough. For years, I kept visualising that scene over and over. When we get rejected in any area of our lives, we personalise it. We keep playing it over and over in our heads. We are quick to ask, 'Why me'? - a question that showcases our inner pride.

When I got home, my mum suggested that I should take up my second choice – an offer to study English language. I wondered, how a *'whole me'* (an aspiring lawyer) would study English. After a few days of reflection, I said it was okay. At that point, I was getting depressed. When we are rejected in relationships, careers, and business, it might feel like the end of the world - just because we get a 'NO!' You will agree that rejection stings; it's painful no matter how minute. Rejection hurts.

Interestingly, I got to the other university only to discover that registration for the new semester had closed for new students. I had even missed the matriculation ceremony. It felt like heaven was against me - everything seemed to work against me. Nevertheless, the authorities advised us to keep coming every day because the registration portal might be briefly reopened. After nothing had happened for the first three days, I said to myself that I was no longer interested - there was no point.

I was rejected not just once but twice. But that was not the end of me. Against all odds, I am a fully qualified lawyer today. In this chapter, I will share with you some tips for overcoming rejection and not sitting or wallowing in hopelessness, feeling undeserving, or unqualified. One thing rejection does is that it creates a fear of trying again. There is always light at the end of the tunnel; rejection is not the end. There are lots of benefits to going through rejection.

Let's read through the Bible about someone who has been rejected several times. He is someone we all know, JESUS. Jesus was rejected too:

'Afterward, Jesus left Capernaum and returned with his disciples to Nazareth, his hometown. On the Sabbath, he went to teach in the synagogue. Everyone who heard his teaching was overwhelmed with astonishment. They said among themselves, "What incredible wisdom has been given to him! Where did he receive such profound insights? And what mighty miracles flow through his hands! Isn't this Mary's son, the carpenter, the brother of Jacob, Joseph, Judah, and Simon? And don't his sisters all live here in Nazareth?" And they took offense at him. Jesus said to them, "A prophet is treated with honor everywhere except in his own hometown, among his relatives, and in his own house." He was unable to do any great miracle in Nazareth, except to heal a few sick people by laying his hands upon them. He was amazed at the depth of their unbelief! Then Jesus went

out into the different villages and taught the people'. - Mark 6:1-6 TPT

Jesus was rejected in Nazareth. Rejection is only sometimes external, as was in my case. It can also be internal - as close as your very thoughts. Jesus returned to His hometown after working miracles in every place He went to and was there to share the power at work in Him. He went into the synagogue to teach, and everyone who heard His teaching was astonished. It was like going for an interview and impressing everyone on the panel with your qualifications, so you should get the job. They acknowledged the wisdom of Jesus, yet they rejected His person. That means, sometimes, rejection is not a reflection of your worth. Sometimes, being rejected does not mean you are worthless; it does not mean that there is nothing good that will come out of you.

People can see the value in you or your intelligence and still say no to you. They acknowledged Jesus' wisdom, and they acknowledged that He worked great miracles, so there was no dispute about His qualification. It was not a dispute about how good He was, it was not a dispute about the value He could add. Rejection, sometimes, can be in isolated places, but it doesn't mean you are getting rejected in every area of your life.

In verses 1-6 of Mark 6, Jesus returned to where He was known, but the people still took offence at Him. That didn't stop Jesus. In verse 7, Jesus gathered His disciples and gave them authority to go out and cast out devils. He told them they did not need too many things; they were to take their staff, and everything they needed would be provided. In verse 11, He told them that as they go into the world, they will experience rejection just as He had experienced rejection. *'Whatever community does not welcome you or receive your message, leave it behind. And as you go, shake the dust off your feet as a testimony against them'* (Mark 6:11 TPT). This put in their consciousness that there will be rejection even though they had authority. These are people coming with the authority in the name of Jesus. He told them that regardless of this authority backing them up, they will go to some places where they won't be accepted. That is the same thing for every one of us; rejection is a part of life. There are places you will go and the doors you will knock on won't grant you access.

There are times when rejection is not tied to your qualification. Rejection is not a reflection of you not doing well; it's just people saying it's not a proper fit. There are instances where rejection is actually due to our lack of preparation and insight. Like in my story, I was rejected because I lacked the right qualifications. It wouldn't have mattered that they changed their requirements during the process if I had the appropriate grade.

The reasons we experience rejection include poor timing, lack of information, lack of necessary qualifications, and in some cases, God just saying no. There are times when rejection is a way of God redirecting our footsteps. Some rejections are divine interruptions.

Let me share another story of my life about rejection. Some years ago, I applied for a position on the global team in my organisation. I was a thriving regional manager at that time, but I was rejected and felt bad. After a period of reflection, I realised I was not qualified for the position I was applying for. Sometimes, we experience rejection because we are not ready for what we are aiming for. Regardless of the multiple reasons we experience rejection, one thing is consistent - the unhealthy feeling that comes with the belief that we are qualified and entitled to it. We can't deal with that bitterness or envy until we ask ourselves or reflect on why we were rejected and be honest with ourselves. One of the pitfalls we encounter is this 'victim mentality', where we take rejection as our identity. We learn to be helpless, and sometimes, we stop trying. We stop believing. By default, we dwell on that rejection – 'Since they told me NO, I am not moving forward' – rather than use it as an opportunity to learn and grow. We adopt that victim mentality that dwells on rejection.

Rejection brings the emotions of inadequacy or not feeling good enough but you should not dwell in rejection. When you dwell on rejection, the benefits that should come out of that experience and the growth opportunities are lost to you. The opportunities for redirection, growth, and learning are lost when we let rejection paralyse us. Jesus didn't sit in that trap. In Jesus' case, He was without fault. He had every qualification and He could back up the miracles He performed. Some of us cannot back up the things we apply for. Jesus could do that and despite all of these, He was rejected. He still moved on and sent His disciples forth. He told His disciples to expect 'no' and not dwell in self-pity. Don't stay there! Shake it off and move on. Shaking it off is not that easy though.

It's not easy to shake it off but when you ask yourself why you were rejected and answer honestly, you will find the strength and courage to shake it off. This will allow you to grow out of rejection. Rejection can be a growth agent for the next level. If this university had not turned me down, I would probably not have attended my alma mater and I would not have met my husband. If I had married a different man, my journey would have been harder. So, I got the right person because I was in the right place. I would say my rejection was a divine interruption. The reality is that when experiencing rejection, we are oblivious to the fact that it can make us better; we just don't see the possibilities. It's only in hindsight that we see the benefits of rejection.

Sometimes, rejection could be a result of a spiritual attack. When there is a recurring pattern where things come easy for everyone else, but when it gets to you, the door is shut; this could be the spirit of rejection at work. You must address this in the place of prayer. The good news is that there is no impossibility with God. The Bible says that *'Wherefore God also hath highly exalted him, and given him a name which is above every name, That at the name of Jesus every knee should bow, of things in heaven, and things in earth, and things under the earth'* (Philippians 2:9-10 KJV). This includes the spirit of rejection. That is the privilege we have in Christ, but everything starts from acknowledging or identifying your emotions of rejection. You cannot move on to see why you experienced rejection until you acknowledge your anger and sadness over it. The first thing is to recognise it; the next is to evaluate the 'why'. Understanding the 'why' of rejection will help you move forward. If your 'why' is that you missed one documentation, then you know what to do. Until you understand 'why', you will not know the next step, someone said, 'God broke my heart so that He could blow my mind'.

So sometimes, rejection might be a divine interruption. There is a principle called *Learned Helplessness* that happens to people who have gone through difficult psychological situations. Helplessness is a learned thing. Some people have been mocked, bullied, and laughed at on stage and they concluded that they will never try again. This is because your brain releases a lot of chemicals that produce the effect of pain so that the pain is as real as physical pain. So, you learn avoidance, you don't want to repeat that thing. That is what happens to people who are addicts of drugs, pornography, or other sinful habits. When they fall over and over again, they just give up. They lose hope and accept that *this is me, this is my weakness* and *I am not good enough*. Rejection can make you minimise yourself more and refuse to stretch yourself. You just get into that cycle of not trying so as to avoid the pain of rejection again.

The first step in overcoming rejection is knowing your worth and value. Rejection makes you feel you're not good enough. You stop trying because you don't want to feel the pain again. The feeling of rejection is like when you touch a hot plate, instinctively you move away, and next time you wouldn't want to touch it. For example, you post on social media, and no one acknowledges it, so you don't want to post anything else because of the pain or the sting. So, the fear of rejection limits us.

How do We Overcome Rejection?

- **Acknowledge your emotions** – There is no need to fake things, admit the fact that you feel rejected.
- **Evaluate the emotion** – it's important that you evaluate. If you don't evaluate the reason for the rejection, you will take it personally. You need to

understand that rejection is a reflection of the situation, it's not a measure of your worth. In the same way, the fear of rejection is learnt, you can also learn to react positively to rejection.

- **Know your identity** - You need to know your identity in God so that you are not defined by rejection. If you don't know your identity, anytime someone tells you that you are not good enough, you will accept and internalise it. You need to let your identity in God define you, not the rejection. If you believe God cannot fail, why can't you believe that rejection is tied to the purpose He has ordained for you? Why do you believe that rejection can change your identity? When you know your identity in Christ, you understand that rejection might be a form of protection. Have a mindset change. Let your identity not be tied to the doctrine you were brought up with. You are deserving of the good things life has to offer. Your identity is tied to what God's Word says about you.
- **Learn from rejection** – Rejection can be a great catalyst to progress. Rejection can offer you the information you need for the next level. What it does is that it tells us what not to do or what to do differently. There is information in every rejection for the next level. When you lose that information, let no experience you go through ever go to waste. Learn something new from your experiences including

painful ones. Learn to use rejection as a catalyst for the next level. Every rejection I have experienced actually prepared me for a higher level. My husband told me that for him every No he hears means next and the next opportunity is always greater.

Psalms 118:22 (KJV) says,
'The stone which the builders refused is become the head stone of the corner'.

Wherever you have been rejected, you are coming back as the headstone, maybe not in that location but wherever you go.

So keep coming to him who is the Living Stone —though he was rejected and discarded by men but chosen by God and is priceless in God's sight. (1 Peter 2:4 TPT)

You might have been rejected by people, God says, '*I will choose you for great honour*'. Rejection shouldn't limit you; rejection should not make you feel unworthy. Rather, identify your emotions and evaluate your rejection and after that, go back to God and pray because your identity is in God. Go back knowing that rejection is just a catalyst to higher places. Above all, find the information you need in the rejection.

Redirecting Your Rejection

One thing I have learnt in life is that many times we are at particular places in our lives which seem like we are doing what we are meant to be doing or the right fit for us. We feel we are in the right circle, however, those places or those people are actually sometimes limiting our growth, limiting our potential. Then God looks at you and says, *'The purpose I have for you is bigger than this location. The purpose I have for you to fulfill is bigger than this'* so God redirects you to take you to the place where you will thrive. When such situations happen, it might seem as if doors are shut against us. The things that seem to be easy for others become difficult for us. I want you to know that it is simply God stepping in and causing doors to shut against you because this is not the right place for you; the growth that you have inside of you is bigger than that location. God is causing people to turn down your applications because your journey of purpose will be difficult if you go through that particular door. It might not be easy but one thing we have the assurance of is that it didn't start with us. We will look at some examples of people who were rejected but whose rejections were God's redirection in their journey of purpose. He had an assignment for them that was greater than where they were positioned. The process of God's redirection is really not pretty.

One story in the Bible that illustrates rejection as a form of redirection is the story of Joseph. Joseph was the second to the last born of his family, he was loved by his father but at the same time, the people that should care for him hated him. His older brothers – who had gone ahead of him and should speak up for him, defend him, guide him, keep the door open for him, and approve him for the next level – rejected him. They rejected him as a brother and even rejected him as an Israelite and sold him out of the nation. In the course of the story, Joseph did not suffer just one rejection He suffered multiple rejections even though he was thriving. Sometimes, you have all it takes like Joseph who was handsome, smart, and could interpret dreams yet he suffered rejections in different phases of his life. But as we go on to the end of the story, we realise that the rejections Joseph suffered were so that he could be positioned rightly for destiny.

Nothing would have moved Joseph from the land of Israel to Egypt to be in control when the famine started except the rejections He suffered. The rejection was so he could be in place to meet the needs of not just his own family but his nation. God's redirection is to fulfill a purpose that we do not know. God is the One who knows the end of a thing even from the beginning. He knows where you should be in the next five years, but if you go through this path, you won't be ready, you won't have the experience of how to manage rejection, and you will not know the strength inside of you. Sometimes, rejection helps us know the strength inside of us. God says His strength is made perfect in our weakness. When we are rejected, when we are at the lowest place, then we identify the strength we never knew we had. God knows you need that strength to redirect your journey a few years in the future.

It's easy to talk about Joseph because we know how it ended but as for me and you, our stories are not yet done. We might be in the process of redirection; God might have redirected us a year or two ago. Sometimes, God delays some things we are asking for because the favour we need for the next level is not available at that time.

In another story in the Bible, someone else got rejected because he was stubborn to do what God had asked him to do. This is someone who God had told what He wanted to do and he said he wouldn't do it. He tried to go a different path and was rejected. Even when people wanted to help him, they couldn't help him because, in the process of helping him, they were losing their lives, losing their resources, and at the end of the day they had to shut the door on him. Can you relate to that? There are people you have been getting along with so well, you entered into business with them and it's thriving, and suddenly the partnership breaks. Sometimes, God had already told you what to do and you have refused, so God jumps in so that you don't spend 40 years in the wilderness like the children of Israel. Their journey was that long simply because of stubbornness. The gentleman I am talking about is Jonah. His story is a very popular story in the Bible. God sent him to a place and he chose a different path on a boat with businessmen who were thriving. They seemed like the right people to work with; you are surrounded by people that have the information that you need, therefore you can go on this journey with them.

Jonah felt he could journey with them but because of his presence in their midst, every single one of them lost their resources. God looked at Jonah and saw the importance of interrupting his journey because there is an end game that is not visible to him. Being thrown out is a form of rejection. Sometimes, in an attempt to help you, people keep you staying at the spot where you are rejected for too long. Sometimes, we know that God is the One telling us that we need to let go of that job because He has something bigger for us, or we need to let go of the relationship because this is not what He has for us. God makes it clear through mentors, visions, His Word, and multiple means.

Jonah was thrown out because God wanted to redirect him and because of his stubbornness, he had to spend three days in the belly of the fish. God redirects us by causing doors to be shut in our faces, by difficulties on our path, by the loss of a very important relationship, and so on. Not every rejection is a redirection. That is why you need to evaluate why you were rejected. If it is a timing thing, you will need to wait for the right time. If it is a lack of qualification or preparation, you will need to do the right thing and if it is a spiritual attack, you will need to tackle it in the place of prayer.

The last story I will share is the story of the four leprous guys at the gate of the city during a severe famine. In the Old Testament, anyone who was leprous was usually cast out. They are not found worthy to be among the people, so they are sent out of the gate. This was the case of these four leprous guys and they must have been lamenting. As we go through the story, we realise that they were positioned where they were because God needed them to be there; they were the ones who informed others that there was abundance just right outside their gate. No one else would have come out of that gate but they were positioned there. I saw something on social media that resonates with me, it said *'Anytime I thought I was being rejected for something good, God was redirecting me to something better'*. That is actually one of the things my husband lives by, that man is strong. Every NO is a NEXT for him and it's always something better.

Being rejected is not the end of your story, your story isn't actually finished. Rejection is a sign that you are stepping out of your comfort zone and trying to attain greater heights. When that rejection is God redirecting you, the end will be more beautiful than the beginning or the middle of the journey. So, be empowered when it is God redirecting you. How do you know it is not just rejection and it is God's redirection? How do you know that this job you were not granted is God directing you to a better place? How do you know that every relationship that has hurt you is actually going to lead you to your true partner? How do you know it is God redirecting you?

I am going to share a few tips:

- The first way you can learn that it is God redirecting you is through sensitivity. When it comes from a place of you being sensitive, not you being dogmatic; being sensitive and open to know that God can come through different means and different directions. You have to know God's voice and you only know the voice of God through constant relationship. God can speak to you in different ways but you can only know if it is God's redirection and that rejection is not an endgame but a doorway to greater opportunities by having a relationship with God. When you have that relationship with God, know His voice, and are sensitive to it, you can go through any season of life.

- The second thing is the place of mentoring and wisdom. Some spiritual leaders can give you wise counsel that will help you know whether God is giving you a lifeline so you can change your position or know if it is the right time for the step, or if you need to do something different.

- Above all, one of the ways to identify it is God is that we shake off the rejection and actually look around and see other opportunities because when God shuts one door He opens other doors, if only you will look and see. If you are not seeing any opportunities or any ways you can re-strategise and rebrand yourself, then you might need to come to the drawing table and ask if this is really God. Jonah was thrown into the belly of the fish but God didn't leave him there. Even after the rejection, he knew what next to do. God doesn't redirect you without being open to communicating with you about other opportunities.

The scriptures say: *'But he said to me, "My grace is sufficient for you, for my power is made perfect in weakness." Therefore, I will boast all the more gladly about my weaknesses, so that Christ's power may rest on me'*. (2 Corinthians 12:9 NIV). Sometimes, without rejection, we don't discover the strength that we need for the journey ahead. Let me tell you this, it doesn't matter how ugly the period of rejection is, it doesn't matter how painful it is to lose a relationship you have invested so much into, it doesn't matter how scary and uncertain it feels to lose your job and source of income. The Bible says in Habakkuk 2:3 (KJV), *'For the vision is yet for an appointed time, but at the end it shall speak, and not lie: though it tarry, wait for it; because it will surely come, it will not tarry'*. Not every rejection is God's redirection, you have to evaluate and be sure.

Rejection as Protection

I was listening to a preacher recently who was talking about the story of Jacob, Leah, and Rachel. It's another well-known Bible story. In this story, Jacob wanted Rachel, and Laban told him to serve for seven years, after which he tricked Jacob and gave him Leah instead. Jacob loved Rachel, so Laban asked him to serve another seven years and he did for Rachel. By the time he married Rachel, he had been married to Leah for seven years. The Bible says that Jacob loved Rachel more than Leah and it was clear she was not wanted because he agreed to go into hard labour for another seven years for Rachel. Leah was rejected, she was not found worthy of being Jacob's wife and it took me a while to find out how that was a protection for the lineage of Leah.

If you read the lineage of Jesus in Matthew 1, Jesus came from the lineage of Judah and Judah was a son of Leah. The rejection Leah suffered was to protect that lineage that will come out of her. Jacob rejected Leah as his wife and because of that rejection God looked at Leah and favoured her. The Bible says God opened Leah's womb because she was hated and rejected. The first son she had was directly tied to her rejection. God closed the womb of Rachel and opened the womb of Leah because she was rejected. Even when the stone is rejected, before God you are chosen as the head of the corner. When Leah was having her children, she was expecting her husband to find her worthy and love her. God had compassion on Leah and even though Rachel was the favoured one at that time, there was Jesus coming out of the lineage of the rejected one. There are some rejections you may have suffered in your life because there is a purpose that will birth greatness in your future. You might not see it or feel like it now. Leah would not have thought of it but her lineage had to bring someone that will not just be successful but will have an everlasting impact. Her rejection was a form of protection for her because her womb was opened and because of that God covered her shame.

Another example could be the story of Moses. His mother threw him out because he needed to be shielded and protected but she knew she couldn't do it effectively. People will feel the child was abandoned, that was what Pharaoh's daughter thought but he wasn't abandoned, he was actually protected. Whatever rejection you might be facing, when you go back to the place of prayers, you will know if it is God when you have a relationship with Him, when you can pick His voice in the midst of a thousand voices. That voice helps you to know God is redirecting and rewriting your story, protecting you until you are able to stand for yourself.

Rejection is painful but rejection can be a catalyst for your growth. Not all pains are bad. Some pains are necessary. No mother brings forth a child without a form of pain, you cannot birth a future of lasting impact without some form of pain. You must be able to look at it and say, *'This is the information I need for the next level'*. You need to evaluate and find the information in that rejection. The earlier you realise that it is God redirecting or protecting you, the faster you reposition yourself and be where God needs you to be, thereby going to the next level you need to be. If

God is protecting you because of rejection now, I am telling you that what He is birthing in your future is greater than what you can think or imagine.

Sometimes, you may experience rejection in your place of destiny, sometimes your rejection may just be a lesson on persistence. It is very important to ask God WHY when we are rejected. Ask, *'What are you teaching me? Is this a detour to somewhere else or do I exercise patience'*? Seek clarity from God. If you are in a dark place where you are not hearing anything from God and your season or journey is still not clear to you, don't suffer in silence. Seek help.

3
FEAR AND ANXIETY

≈≈≈

FEAR AND ANXIETY ARE rarely talked about in the Christian Community today but a lot of people suffer from fear and anxiety which makes it a very essential subject of discussion.

Fear and anxiety are often used interchangeably but they are not the same, though their symptoms are quite similar. The major difference between fear and anxiety is that fear relates to a known danger, it relates to something that is known, and there is a clear threat. Fear is a feeling of stress and worry which is excessive about something that is known or understood. While anxiety, on the other hand, arises from an unknown or poorly defined threat. People with anxiety can't pinpoint what exactly the thing is, they can't talk about triggers, they cannot talk about things that bother them or define the threat.

Anxiety is more than feeling stressed or worried. We all feel worried, worry is what protects us. You have to feel a little bit of worry in your daily life to keep yourself going. Same thing with stress, stress is what wakes you up in the morning and gets you to work. You need a little bit of stress and worry to keep going but when stress is much more than that, then you are in the territory of anxiety.

While stress is a common response to pressure, it can easily aggravate from the first phase (arousal stress) which is normal to a more intense second phase (distress). This second phase is the phase of anxiety. Everyone feels anxious from time to time, but not everybody that feels anxious has anxiety just like not everyone that feels fear is fearful. When your anxious feelings don't go away after the stressful situation is gone, when you are anxious without any particular reason, when there is really nothing that you can pinpoint as the cause of the feeling; then you might be suffering from anxiety.

Christians can suffer from anxiety, so the fact that you suffer from anxiety does not make you less of a

Christian. Anxiety is a mental illness and it is not different from migraine or high blood pressure or diabetes or any other illness. The fact that you suffer from anxiety doesn't mean that you don't have faith, it doesn't mean you are carnal, or not spiritual. It is part of your humanity for you to have anxious feelings at times or for you to worry sometimes. If you are a mum, you worry about your kids. If you are a grandma, you worry about your grandkids. Who doesn't worry? Everyone has to have a little bit of worry because that gives you a bit of drive and motivation. Worry is part of bonding, particularly when we worry about people we care about.

It's a natural phenomenon to feel a bit of worry and anxiety from time to time but when those anxious feelings don't go away after the stressful situation has been taken care of – or for no particular reason of your knowledge, you just won't stop feeling anxious – then there is a problem. This is the basis for people who go through Post Traumatic Stress Disorder (PTSD). They have gone through a stressful event and then the stressful event has passed for one year, two years, or three years but they can't stop reliving the moment and that makes them unable to cope with their daily life. Those feelings start to subconsciously interrupt their present relationships because of the conditioning and value tagging from their experience.

Anxiety is very common in the world we live in. Statistics show that one in four people suffer from anxiety. Most of these people are part of the church and not necessarily the world but they suffer in silence.

What is Anxiety?

Anxiety is that diffused, unpleasant sensation of apprehension. People who suffer from anxiety are pressured and have this sense of apprehension. People who suffer from anxiety have this feeling of the worst even though the signs around them don't show the worst. Anxiety is a response to an imprecise or unknown threat; it is like that uneasiness that you feel when you are walking down a dark alley alone even though you have not seen any threat.

Anxiety basically is an irrational fear. When people feel anxiety, it produces a lot of sensations in the body, those sensations are meant to prepare them for a flight or fight response to get them out of that place. Those responses are essential for our survival. The way your body responds to that feeling of anxiety is meant to sort of protect you.

Those symptoms include:

- Increased heart rate. Your heart begins to pound.
- Cold chills on your skin.
- Sweating
- Headaches
- Muscle jerking
- Shortness of breath

When the feeling of apprehension is irrational – you know that there is a bit of pressure building up in you and you can't pinpoint any cause. There is no clear reason for it, or maybe there was a stressor but the stressful event has passed – then you might be suffering from anxiety.

A Test on How Anxious You Have Been in the Last Two Weeks

Not at all -1 Several days - 2 More than half of the days - 3 Nearly every day - 4

- Over the last two weeks, how often have you been feeling nervous, anxious, or on the edge?
- Over the last two weeks, how often have you not been able to control worrying?
- Over the last two weeks, how often have you been worrying too much about different things?
- In the last two weeks, how often have you had trouble relaxing?
- In the last two weeks, how often have you been so restless that it's hard to sit still?
- In the last two weeks, how often have you been easily annoyed or irritable?
- In the last two weeks, how often have you been feeling afraid that something bad is going to happen?

If you sum up all your answers on this scale and you have a score that is more than 14-15, you are already showing signs of anxiety. If your score is over 20, you will need to seek help.

What is Fear?

Fear is an emotional response to a known or identified threat. If you are walking down the dark alley and someone points a gun at you, you should experience fear unless you are *Jack Bauer*. Most people who experience fear will also experience symptoms of anxiety. If you are facing a situation where there is an imminent danger, fear is a natural response. For instance, if you hear a gunshot, the fear you feel is meant to protect you, otherwise, you will become a victim. The emotion of fear is a protective emotion, the problem is when the emotion of fear persists after the stressful situation is gone or when the emotion of fear rises or persists when the trigger itself is gone. Sometimes, there are things in our life that produce fear that we cannot get rid of.

Strategies to Handle Fear and Anxiety

For Anxiety:

1. Pursuing a healthy lifestyle

When we pursue healthy relationships with our friends and family, when we eat well and sleep well, we are active and we enjoy nature. All of these activities help to reduce our stress levels.

2. Getting to know yourself and what your vulnerabilities are

There is no point living in denial, if you have got these persistent feelings then there is no point denying them. That is the way you are wired. You have to be intentional about making good use of what you have and trying to maximise your strengths while minimising your weaknesses. Your anxieties show you are a broken vessel, they show your vulnerabilities as a human being and that you have to depend on God. Every time you feel anxiety, it's a sign that you are human and you have to lean on God. Don't let that define you or define your spirituality. You have to own it, that you are broken clay that God is making a masterpiece with.

3. Journaling

This is very therapeutic, it's a very useful tool because it reminds you of who you are. Every Christian should journal about the things that God has told them about who they are. This will boost your self-esteem and make you see yourself in the right way.

4. Deep breaths

When you take deep breaths when you are nervous, you are trying to calm your hormones down. When we are in a very excited state, our minds are only prepared to fight or fly, so we cannot really think about things deeply. You cannot innovate, be creative, or even hear from God clearly when in that state. You can't thrive in an atmosphere of anxiety. If you are extremely anxious before a presentation, take deep breaths as you count to three, and exercise your diaphragm. it is very important as it helps you to relax.

5. Developing a relationship with God

God loves it when we are vulnerable; be open and go to God just the way you are. Tell Him that you need encouragement and hope. God will accept you the way you are and He won't push you aside. Develop a robust relationship with God. This is what unbelievers don't have and why Christians should not live in a perpetual state of fear and anxiety. We should thrive. Your spirituality gives you an open door to thrive above fear and anxiety. Your spirituality is a means to dominance, dominating that state of fear and anxiety.

Psalms 119:165 (NKJV) says,

Great peace have those who love Your law, And nothing causes them to stumble.

2 Timothy 1:7 (KJV) says,

For God hath not given us the spirit of fear; but of power, and of love, and of a sound mind.

As you focus on developing a robust relationship with God or you spend time meditating on His Word and in prayers, you experience what the scriptures above say. The Word of God renews your mind which is where anxiety manifests.

In Mathew Chapter 26, Jesus in the Garden of Gethsemane went through a terrible situation of anxiety about His death. That shows the humanity of Jesus. Jesus prayed and the capillaries ruptured on His skin so that He was sweating blood. He was under immense stress. Jesus didn't walk comfortably to the cross. He was sorrowful to the point of death; He was in emotional agony. Jesus needed strength. He prayed, and the God sent angels to strengthen Him.

Our spirituality should open a way up to overcome our anxiety. The fact that you are anxious doesn't mean you are not spiritual, it means that you have to lean on God and He will strengthen you to overcome it just like Jesus did.

6. The power of meditation

1 Timothy 4:13, 15 (KJV) says,

Till I come, give attendance to reading, to exhortation, to doctrine. Meditate upon these things; give thyself wholly to them; that thy profiting may appear to all.

Meditation is really important; it is not just reading the Bible. Meditation is like taking a scripture and going over it again and again in your mind while lying on your bed, walking, or at your job. It's on the bed of meditation that revelation is formed. While you meditate, insights and inspiration come. People that don't meditate don't get inspired; they don't get novel ideas.

7. Associating with people

'*Not forsaking the assembling of ourselves together...*' (Hebrews 10:25 NKJV)

We need other people especially when we are facing challenges. The Bible said in Ecclesiastes 4:9-10, '*Two are better than one, Because they have a good reward for their labour. For if they fall, one will lift up his companion. But woe to him who is alone when he falls, For he has no one to help him up*'.

Leaning on other people is very essential. If you are feeling anxious, you can talk to someone. It could be a trained counsellor, a family member, a pastor, a mentor, etc. Just talk to someone. If you are married, talk to your spouse about your feelings. Don't try to suppress them. Be vulnerable. If you are going to talk to someone, talk to God at least about it.

4
LONELINESS

≈≈≈

LONELINESS IS A FEELING of isolation and separation from others. I believe everyone reading this right now has gone through a stage of their life when they had that feeling of isolation, feeling of being away from others. It may be because of your background, skin colour, or your beliefs. You may not be accepted because of the way you talk, think and act. It may be that your attitude or energy does not sync, or you are not accepted by the people around you. Loneliness can also be a result of physical separation because of migration. You can feel lonely or isolated when you do not have that physical contact with the people you love.

Sometimes, people can be lonely in a place where there are a lot of people. It's still possible for you to be lonely in a room full of people. You can be in a room full of people and still feel disconnected. You can be amongst family or friends and still not get that feeling of love.

You deserve to be loved but the reality is that life happens and many people may find themselves in a situation where they make contact physically with people and don't still get that vibe or energy that they really want. You might be married and your connection with your spouse is slowly dying as the days go by. You may be at work on a team and it feels like you are running on your own, it doesn't feel like a team sport anymore. It looks like you are just by yourself and you are going solo because you are not getting support. It may be that you are not getting any encouragement from anyone; all they do is criticise you, and no one seems to affirm you or give you any praise. All they see are errors, inadequacies, and mistakes. That can make you feel lonely. It is possible to be in contact with people and still be lonely.

Loneliness sometimes arises from our fear of abandonment. You see that in a baby who is beginning to recognise the face of their parents. When that parent, whether mum or dad, leaves that baby alone for a second – even if that baby is put in the custody of a relative who will look after them – the baby will immediately experience fear and cry. People call it 'stranger anxiety'. The reality is that at that point, the baby was feeling lonely. They may be in contact with their grandmother or a neighbour but then feel abandoned by the person who loves them. Often, we feel lonely because of the fear of abandonment, the fear of disapproval, and the fear of not being good enough.

Loneliness can vary from mild feelings of isolation to severe forms which can become problematic and end up leading to depression and anxiety. One of the symptoms of depression is profound loneliness. The reality is that God has created us to be social beings and God has put in our DNA a wanting to be loved. God has created you as a social being, God has not created you to be in isolation. God saw Adam and said it is not good for man to be alone as seen in Genesis 2:18 (KJV), *'And the Lord God said, It is not good that the man should be alone; I will make him an help meet for him'*.

Ecclesiastes 4:9-12
'[9]Two are better than one; because they have a good reward for their labour. [10]For if they fall, the one will lift up his fellow: but woe to him that is alone when he falls; for he has not another to help him up. [11]Again, if two lie together, then they have heat: but how can one be warm alone? [12]And if one prevail against him, two shall withstand him; and a threefold cord is not quickly broken'.

God has genetically pre-programmed us to be social beings. Most of us require this kind of social contact to a certain degree. Some other people only need a little bit of contact and are more introverted. Others are very expressive and extroverted and would like to have much more contact with people. Whatever the case, God hasn't created us to be in isolation.

Does God understand my loneliness? Yes, He does. Does God care? Yes, He cares. *'Seeing then that we have a great High Priest who has passed through the heavens, Jesus the Son of God, let us hold fast our confession. For we do not have a High Priest who cannot sympathize with our weaknesses, but was in all points tempted as we are, yet without sin. Let us therefore come boldly to the throne of grace, that we may obtain mercy and find grace to help in time of need'.* Hebrews 4:14-16 (NKJV)

God cares. God understands your loneliness, but the reality is that even though God has created you to be a social person; to be loved, to be a blessing to others, and be blessed by others. There are times life happens. Situations come, transitions occur, people come into our lives and they go away, we lose loved ones, and people move away and move on. Sometimes, we feel lonely because we don't let go. When bad situations happen, they can cause a social separation, they can make us feel that we are not good enough and all of these can inevitably lead us to that feeling of loneliness. This is not a pity party, yours is not the worst of trials. I am not writing to whip up sympathy for you but to share with you that though I know you are lonely, and that can be crippling. However, that is not the worst of trials.

When you go to the scriptures, you find the story of Joseph who was betrayed by his brothers and for about 12 years, Joseph was in the prison (judging by the fact that he was 17 years old when he was sold into slavery by his brothers and spent about one year in Potiphar's house before he was thrown into prison). Joseph, who was put in charge of prison affairs, only had two people that could be called friends (because of his conversation with them that was recorded) for those twelve years - the butler and the baker (whom he met towards the end of his stay in the prison). The baker was beheaded, the butler left the prison but forgot him for at least two more years, even though Joseph specifically told him about his predicament and asked that he spoke to Pharaoh on his behalf. This guy was in solitary confinement for a long time, so just imagine the memories he could have had.

Sometimes when you are lonely, you remember the good old days. Loneliness is not a new phenomenon. Moses was a prince in Egypt, yet he was lonely. He saw the Israelites and knew he didn't belong in the palace. When he tried to help God by saving an Israelite who was maltreated by an Egyptian, he found himself as a reclusive shepherd for 40 years in the wilderness. The same Moses was an Egyptian prince. Moses had been broken down. So, don't tell me your problems are unique. John the Baptist was in the wilderness eating locust and honey and dressed in the skin of a donkey, preaching the gospel as hard and raw, *'Repent for the kingdom of God is at hand'*. When he preached a message that King Herod did not like, he arrested him and put him in prison; from the wilderness to the prison.

You are not alone in your loneliness (no matter how unique you think it is) is what I am trying to say. So many great people have gone through that same process, and so many great people have been lonely. Jesus, Himself, was like a celebrity in His time. He could be walking along the road and a multitude of people will start following him. Some will bring their sick to be healed and Jesus would work so many miracles but when it was time to die, Jesus died alone.

Even His disciples ran away. While on the cross, Jesus said, *'My Father why have you forsaken me'*. God turned His eyes from Jesus for the very first time because Jesus was loaded with the sins of the world.

Do you know that Paul, one of the greatest evangelists of all time, spent more time in prison than any other person in the Scripture? Paul was unashamed till the very end. There was a time Paul was arrested in Rome and He spent two years under house arrest. What happened to Paul at the end of the day? Paul did not compromise his stand in spite of all the persecutions. How I wish you will have the same attitude.

The woman with the issue of blood was a woman who bled constantly for twelve years. I just can't get my head around that. She was ceremonially unclean. Do you know what it means to live in a culture where people regarded you as unclean and unaccepted? She was rejected by society and defined as awkward or odd. Any furniture she touches becomes unclean, every single thing and person she touches becomes unclean. Look at the extent to which she would have felt alone and isolated.

People have a lot of wrong ideas about loneliness. Some feel loneliness is a sign of immaturity and weakness. That is not true. Loneliness is not weakness or immaturity. There are a lot of people who are at the top of the pyramid and are lonely because that space is not crowded. The bottom is where it is crowded. The reason why a lot of celebrities live empty lives is that deep down within them, they are empty and they have to put up an act every single time. They have to undergo plastic surgery and apply fillers to keep themselves younger. Loneliness is not a sign of immaturity. It's human to feel lonely from time to time. Jesus was in the Garden of Gethsemane and He felt so alone. It's not wrong to feel lonely.

Every time you feel lonely, it's time for a change. Loneliness is a signal and a characteristic of change. Anytime you feel lonely, it's because God wants you to do something different. Loneliness is a time for growth. Loneliness is a signal that it's time to grow. You feel lonely because your brain and your mind are not getting satisfaction where you are. It's time to stretch yourself.

'We tend to do most of our growing only when we are provoked by pain, discomfort or crisis of one kind or the other' – John Selby

Fake Solutions to Loneliness

1. Rebound Relationship

One mistake to avoid when you feel lonely after a breakup is going into a rebound relationship. It is natural to want to jump into another relationship to ease the pain or to show that person you have moved on and that you are good enough. A rebound relationship is not a solid relationship because it does not allow a lot of emotional healing. It doesn't allow a lot of spiritual perspectives. A lot of times when people jump into relationships like that, they make mistakes. Rebound relationships may soothe you temporarily but in the long run, it's not going to give you that permanent sense of satisfaction. It may leave you in a worse state than you were before.

2. Bad Habits

Bad habits like eating too much, drinking, watching too much TV, or sitting and doing nothing will not take away your loneliness, at least not for long. They won't solve the problem; they only hide it for a while.

Real Solutions to Loneliness

1. Direct your thinking to others - If you learn to direct your thinking to other people when you are in a state of loneliness, you will learn to thrive above that. Look for opportunities to be a blessing to other people. When you start to feel lonely, call others. Reach out to other people. When you feel lonely, look away from yourself and help other people. Show some love to other people.

2. Determine that you can control your reaction but you can't control all the circumstances that come your way - A lot of times, what you go through might not be under your control. At this time, you must pray, and ask God to fill you with love and joy. You may not be able to control all that happens to you.

3. Smile, laugh, and be friendly - Learn to find a way to manage stress. Watch healthy comedies that would lighten the mood. Learn to just laugh, smile and relieve stress.

4. Go to church - This is not the time to stay away from the church. This is the time for you to connect.

5. Adopt a pet (for animal lovers) - If you are someone who loves animals, then this may be a good time to have one as a pet. Expending your energy on and directing your emotions towards the pet can help you come out of loneliness.

6. Volunteer - Giving yourself to another course can be of great help. It helps you divert your energy and focus on the greater good. It's another way of shifting the focus from you to others. Look out for where your help, input, expertise, etc. is needed.

7. Lean on others - God has created us to derive pleasure and satisfaction from other people. Don't just be a loner. Talk about your issues with others.

5
PROCRASTINATION

≈≈≈

PROCRASTINATION IS THE THIEF of time. If we are honest with ourselves and look at our lives, we will realise that procrastination really affects us. I have been on a weight loss journey for quite some time now. One of the requirements is to weigh your meals, calculate your calories, and monitor your calorie intake. So particularly during the lockdown, I just realised that I started procrastinating. I was supposed to measure the calories of each part of a meal because all the different meal components have different calorie contents. I already knew how many calories I needed in a day, so all I needed to do was ensure a balance. I also needed to ensure that my carbs and protein were balanced.

After a while, it was a struggle, and I started procrastinating. Finally, I started letting it go. I will always say, 'I will do it tomorrow'. So, I stopped monitoring my carbs, and I wasn't consistent in weighing myself. I had a gym membership that was paid for by direct debit. Whenever I saw the deductions, I would feel bad, but when it came to the time to go to the gym, I would always say, 'I will go tomorrow'. When tomorrow comes, there are still excuses, and I will settle for next week.

It's easy to go into this perpetual cycle of procrastination characterised by guilt feelings, self-doubt, and so on. Most procrastinators get to the point where they start doubting themselves. They actually lose confidence in their ability to stick to a particular task. For instance, when you go to the doctor or your physiotherapist, and he asks you to do an exercise right there in the room, you already doubt that you will follow through. So, how did you learn not to trust yourself to stick to the task? Because you have repeated failures over and over again.

Procrastination is a reflection of a lack of self-control. It reflects a breaking of self-regulation. As human beings, God has given every one of us agency over our lives. He has given us self-control to regulate our lives and avoid living our lives based on feelings. When procrastination occurs, there is actually a voluntary downregulation of self-control.

Procrastination is when we voluntarily delay an intended action, despite knowing that we will be worse off for the delay. When you voluntarily delay an important action despite knowing there will be negative consequences for your delay, you are procrastinating. This breakdown occurs when we are faced with a task that will lead to unpleasant feelings. When we delay, we often want to feel good for now or delay the pain of a task for a later time. Procrastination is not the same as laziness. In fact, when we procrastinate, we are often busy. Procrastination is an active process, which means you choose to do something else instead of the task you should be doing.

Procrastination is something that often delays us. How many times have you seen an opportunity and instead of you doing it right there or picking up the phone to make the call, you delay and miss the opportunity? When you act promptly when God gives you an idea or gives you an opportunity, the obedience of taking that initial step will open more doors. The majority of procrastinators are not lazy, they are just busy doing something else. They are not paying attention enough. Procrastination could also be a symptom of laziness.

See what Proverbs 6:9-11 NIV says,

'How long will you lie there, you sluggard? When will you get up from your sleep? A little sleep, a little slumber, a little folding of the hands to rest— and poverty will come on you like a thief and scarcity like an armed man'.

Proverbs 10:26 (NIV) also says,
'As vinegar to the teeth and smoke to the eyes, so are sluggards to those who send them'.

Another interesting point about procrastination is that it is common to every human. I don't think there is any human that doesn't procrastinate. Every human has or undertakes a measure of procrastination. Research done recently by a renowned psychologist, P.S. Steele, found that 95% of people actually admit to procrastinating. Procrastinating is very common but, of course, it can become a problem when it is limiting you. Many of us do not know how many opportunities we have missed by just not taking that bold step. So, we have to be prompt. Once we recognise God's voice or have an intuition that this is God, we have to take that step and take it in faith because you can never tell what can come out of it. Tim Pychyl is the author of a book called *Solving the Procrastination Puzzle*. He talked about seven types of activities that lead to procrastination:

1. Boring

If you are involved in any activity that is not intellectually stimulating or emotionally engaging enough, you are more likely to procrastinate. For example, I am a doctor who sends out lots of letters every week. I don't type these letters; I dictate and have people transcribe them. I could have fifteen to twenty letters to dictate after a session on a given day. For new patients with complex diseases (such as Parkinson's disease), a comprehensive letter is usually required to capture their medical history. What I realised is that I prefer to dictate shorter letters first. I leave the long boring ones for last, making it easy to procrastinate about them. By the next day, the memory of the patient's details will no longer be fresh in my mind, so a ten-minute dictation ends up taking more than twenty minutes.

2. Frustrating

Frustration is a motivation killer. You will naturally be laid back at doing anything that you have tried doing but have encountered defeat while trying it. It is easy to procrastinate on whatever frustrates you.

3. Difficult

It is very normal to embrace simple tasks or responsibilities while avoiding difficult ones. And in the event that they are not avoidable, the next thing that comes to mind is to delay taking action.

4. Ambiguous

Ambiguity is never a friend of productivity. When people are not sure of what to do or what is expected of them, they become uninterested and will naturally push things till later.

5. Well-structured

Structure helps to enforce discipline and ensure results. This is the reason for having to-do lists, timelines, timetables, reminders, schedules, etc. All of these are tools that help ensure to put a structure that will enhance productivity. Where there is structure, discipline is ensured, hence procrastination is curtailed.

6. Delayed Gratification

Any activity that does not yield an immediate result like gardening, losing weight, or learning a new skill or language can be often procrastinated because the reward is not immediate.

7. Lack of Purpose

Something that lacks personal meaning to you is what you will naturally procrastinate on.

Procrastination can be harmful. When you keep procrastinating, you put pressure on yourself and that leads to feelings of guilt that reduce your productivity. When procrastination becomes a habit, you lose motivation and drive.

How Do We Solve Procrastination?

1. **Reflect** – A lot of self-reflection needs to take place to deal with procrastination. You must reflect and take stock of what you are doing and how you are doing it. Self-reflection brings you to a place of awareness. You can only improve your self-regulation if you are in a position of awareness. So, you have got to sit with yourself and have some self-talk.

2. **Re-access** – You have got to reassess your feelings. What feelings do I have that lead me to procrastinate, and how do I feel when I procrastinate? There are times procrastination might lead you to sin through disobedience. If God asks you to do something and you ignore it or go contrary, that's a sin. So you must reassess the state of your mind.

3. **Re-orientate** - You have got to start, just start. Don't even try to start, just start it. Don't think about how.

'Ants are creatures of little strength, yet they store up their food in the summer'.
Proverbs 30:25 (NIV)

The ants gather food that will help them survive a whole winter because they don't work in winter. If you think about how you are going to survive in winter, that's too big for you. The ants don't think about how to survive a whole winter. They gather one bit of food at a time all the days of summer. When the colony of ants does that in summer, they have enough storage and provision for winter. Commit yourself to little things, and don't get overwhelmed by how complex or tedious things can be. Just start small. By doing it, you also rebuild trust in yourself. Start with the little things, and don't become perplexed over the complex things. Little gains are very important if we are going to have sustainable success. Don't be too concerned about the immediate result; think long-term.

6
EMOTIONAL PAIN

≈≈≈

UNDERSTANDING EMOTIONAL MASTERY STARTS first by understanding how the brain and mind work. TD Jakes once said, '*God gave you a brain so you can give some rest*'. That's true because we often bother God with things our brains can figure out. The primary function of a brain is to keep you alive, and your brain does that by doing two things - minimising threat and maximising reward. So, your brain connects you to the world through your senses and controls your internal processes such as respiration, circulation, etc. Whatever the threat is, your brain wants to minimise it and maximise the reward. So when you are in a threat state, you have negative emotions. Also, when you are in a reward state, you have a lot of positive emotions. However, what is a threat to you may not be a threat to someone else.

The second thing is that although all your sensory experiences get to the brain, you may not be conscious of all of them - they don't really get into the thinking brain immediately. This is because your attention is limited. Your attention is your most prized possession. Perceiving everything around you at all times will make you less productive. Your brain is constantly scanning for threats - up to five times a second. It's a subconscious thing.

We often start to feel before we think. God designed the brain so that we don't have to think about things that are a threat to us before we feel or act on them. There is a gap between feeling and thinking - estimated in duration to be about 80 milliseconds. One of the advantages of emotional mastery is that it can prolong the gap between our feeling and thinking, so we don't act on impulse. It is called cognitive veto. This helps us act differently than we would typically have acted in response to an action.

An illustration of cognitive veto is when your car gets bashed by another vehicle. You get out of your car, ready to give it to the offender, only to realise that they are an army officer. Your response will immediately change from being angry to being amicable. All the anger dissipates once you realise that you can't bully the fellow. Most of us don't act out how we feel, but when the environment feeds our ego, we lash out and act inappropriately. Your brain generates the emotions but the goal of every emotion your brain generates is to keep you alive by minimizing threats and maximizing rewards. On the average, you generate about 150 emotions every hour. However, most of these are subconscious. Now, let me give you my definition of emotion. An *emotion is a subconscious biological response to internal or external events that produces a physiological or behavioural outcome.*

Let me try to break it down. All emotions, when they start, occur subconsciously. It takes a bit of time before you feel the emotion. Actually, it is the outcome of the emotion you feel, not the emotion itself. Emotions are biological responses. They are natural and human. Every human is emotional because we all have emotions. What you are responding to could be internal or external. It could be a response to your hormones, menstrual cycle, pregnancy, etc. Internal and external stimuli generate emotions. The majority of your emotions are not expressed and if they are not expressed in behavioural and physiological form, they are not felt. The anxiety you feel (with racing heartbeats, churning stomach, etc) when you are about to climb the stage is a physiological response to the emotions produced at that point. When someone annoys you, and you get angry - that's only a response to the emotion. It's the physiological outcome of the emotion you feel, which will manifest in your body language or facial expressions. Emotional mastery is all about understanding the outcomes of your emotions because you cannot stop your emotions.

Understanding the physiological responses of that emotion (anger, chest tightness, heartbeats, etc.) defines emotional mastery. That is, you are able to control the effects of that emotion so that you don't remain in the threat state. Remember that in the threat state, you are not productive, your thinking is narrow, and you lack insight. A classic example is the story of Hagar. I wrote a book with some of my mentees titled **Hagar: Unloved and Unwanted**, where we zoomed in on her life. I strongly recommend the book. Hagar was in a threat state. Every major decision in her life was made by others - sold to slavery, became a surrogate mother, impregnated without her consent, etc. She was finally sent away and roamed the wilderness. She had a lot of emotional trauma. Her only hope and future was her son, Ishmael, who was almost dying. Hagar was overwhelmed by her emotions that she couldn't even see that there was a well somewhere near her. She can't be blamed for her overwhelming feelings, though. God came through an angel to call her attention to the well. Her solution was around her. She turned and finally saw the well.

There was a time in my life when I was really in a bad state. My dad left home, and things were terrible. I was angry with my dad, and although I was a tongue-speaking, demon-binding Christian, I just didn't like him. I knew I had crossed the line because I deeply resented him. I was performing well in other areas but knew I wasn't at my peak. There were many limitations here and there, and there were still things I couldn't do. One day, my father came, and I had a very frank discussion with him. I was sincere with him. I told him I hoped he knew I didn't like him. We had a long conversation, and I was able to let out my emotions. Shortly after that, my dad became sick and sadly passed away. But I will never forget the day on his sick bed when he said to me, *'Niyi, I love you'*. I know of people who are in such a state. They are very active and effective, but deep down, they are unhappy.

You will never be at your peak performance when your emotions get the best of you. When you are in a threat state, you can't see opportunities. You may do a lot of prayers but you cannot hear God. When you're in a threat state, the soul-spirit connection is reduced.

Nobody can control an emotion; it is the outcome of the emotion that you should seek to regulate.

How to Regulate Your Emotions

Your emotions are brief and biological and express themselves through physiological responses. When you think about those emotions and reflect deeply on them, you assign meaning to them, and they become feelings. For example, suppose somebody does something that makes you angry. By repeatedly reflecting on the situation, you may start to develop feelings of hate, disappointment, rejection, and low esteem. When these feelings last for a long time, they become responsible for your mood. For instance, he emotion is anger and short-lived, but now you have attached some meaning to it, usually based on your past experiences. You begin to fill in the gaps, which we are not really good at as humans.

Your brain predicts the future from the past. This is what happens when you are angry. Your past experiences of anger assign meaning to the present state of anger. This generates feelings that last longer. And when feelings last longer, they result in a mood.

Your mood is determined by your feelings, and your feelings are determined by emotion. There are two key strategies for emotional mastery. They are the reactive strategies and the proactive strategies.

Reactive Strategies

Let's say you are now in an emotional state where you have negative feelings. You are not able to perform at your peak but you are still doing stuff. You are still achieving your targets but deep down you know you are in a state of emotional dysregulation. What you need in such an instance are reactive strategies which are, in fact, circuit breakers. One such reactive strategies is BLR (Breathe, Label, Reappraise), which was put together by Kristen Hansen (from Enhansen Performance Australia).

When you exhale, you activate the parasympathetic system of the brain, which helps you to be calm. This kind of deep breathing (6 breaths per minute) can do wonders. The next time you are angry at somebody, chill and take a deep breath. Practice it. It works. It will calm your hormones. I have an app that helps me do that. The next thing you do after taking deep breaths is to label your emotion. You want to ask yourself, 'How am I feeling now'? You don't have to talk out loud. You need to be self-aware. Some people are not self-aware; they just keep on going!

I remember recently being angry with what my son did, and I was fussing about it. Then he asked why I was visibly angry and wondered what the issue was. At first, I thought he was trying to minimise his offence, but then it occurred to me that the case was not worth my anger. Would I have done that to someone else's child? Perhaps I was that angry because I had great expectations of my son. What my son did was what any other kid would do. I eventually labelled the emotions after he left, concluding that I had gone overboard. I was then able to reappraise the situation. If you are a person of faith, this is where an activity such as confessing God's Word comes in.

Proactive Strategies

These are strategies you apply daily to bring subconscious emotions you didn't even feel to your attention. For example, some people get angry, and you won't even notice it in their body language. An excellent proactive strategy is brain break. Your brain operates in a cycle of 90 minutes. It's not humanly possible for your brain to always be at work. In 24 hours, your brain only operates at its peak for just 4 hours. So your brain needs a rest of ten to twenty minutes every ninety minutes. You can take a walk or watch a short video. It's a natural cycle. Other proactive strategies that have been proven useful include exercise, a good diet and mindfulness.

When I was 6, I was abused, but I told no one until I decided to write my first book. Although I was little then, I was conscious of what was happening. I knew it was harmful to me. My wife and I later talked about it, and I also discussed it with my mum (I didn't want her to know about it after reading the book). Did it have an effect on me? Absolutely! When I reflected, I concluded that it affected me in many other ways. If you do not control the way you feel, it may come back to haunt you.

7
DEBT

≈≈≈

IT'S GOD'S DESIRE FOR us to succeed. God wants us to have more than enough; He wants us to be financially independent and robust. God wants us to prosper. To prosper means not living from hand to mouth; to prosper means you have enough for yourself and can be a blessing to others. That's God's desire for us, but a lot of that relies on ourselves as well; a lot of it depends on what we do with the resources that God brings our way. God will bring growth opportunities our way, but how we manage them is crucial.

'Be sure you know the condition of your flocks, give careful attention to your herds; for riches do not endure forever, and a crown is not secure for all generations. When the hay is removed and new growth appears and the grass from the hills is gathered in, the lambs will provide you with clothing, and the goats with the price of a field. You will have plenty of goats' milk to feed your family and to nourish your female servants'. Proverbs 27:23-27 (NIV)

This passage speaks about having a financial plan and strategy. Pay careful attention and put in the effort to understand the state of your flock – understand what your net worth is. What are your assets? Where are you in your finances? In that scripture, you see many principles outlined as follows:

1. The need for diligence

Diligence is essential if you are to successfully implement any plan. You need to monitor the state of your financial situation. You need to know how you spend your money, where you spend your money, and what's happening to your assets. If you ignore this principle of diligently monitoring your finances, you will find yourself making poor decisions and spending money you do not have. It's your responsibility, not God's responsibility, to monitor the state of your flock. Whatever God has given you, it is your job to be diligent in reviewing that. You have got to look at your finances repeatedly to see where you are. If you do not pay enough attention to review the state of your finances, you will get into trouble over and over again. It is your own responsibility to monitor the state of your finances.

2. Accountability

God requires us to be accountable for everything He has given us. You are a treasurer of God's resources. Everything you have now has been provided for you to do whatever you can with it and profit from it.

Understanding Debt

God requires us to be accountable for everything He has given us. You are a treasurer of God. Every time you get a product or are offered a service that you cannot afford to pay for in full, you have to take the credit, which in turn becomes a debt to you. Your credit has a similar buying power to money. There is much more credit in the economy than money. The total amount of physical currency in circulation is minuscule compared to the amount of credit in our economy because the current world system runs on debt.

A lot of Christians don't have an understanding of credit and debt because we have been taught that debt is bad. Debt could be harmful if managed wrongly, but the rich keep getting richer because our current system's growth and productivity are based on credit. That is why it is essential to understand how credit works. If you don't know how credit works, you will think wealth only comes from the income generated from employment or business. That's not often the case. If you believe all the wealth you will have in your life will come from work, earning, saving, and investing, you will lock yourself out of global wealth. In most parts of the world, it is tough to buy a home without getting credit. The average price for residential dwellings in Sydney, where I live, is over a million dollars. How long would you work, earn and save up to a million dollars? What you do is you go to the bank and ask for credit.

It is essential to understand how credit works because if you don't understand, you will have an idea of what the Bible says in Proverbs 22:7, *'The borrower is always a servant to the lender'*. Not to give you a license to go and borrow anyhow, the point is that you must understand how the economy works; how credit is created; what debt is, and how all of that can help you in today's world so that you are not just working, but you can leverage the current systems to create wealth. There is good debt, and there is bad debt.

The Difference between Good Debt and Bad Debt
Any debt that increases your net worth and future value is good. If you take credit to do anything that

builds up your future worth, that is a good debt. Many times, we take debts to increase our productivity or improve our earning power and value. That is a good debt. On the other hand, any debt that you incur that does not improve your net worth or enhance your productivity is not good. Any debt that improves consumption or affords you a luxurious lifestyle is not good and bad debts get you into trouble.

Examples of Good Debts are:
1.   Taking out a mortgage.
Taking out a mortgage is a good debt and of course, good things can be abused. I have seen people who took mortgages to buy houses that are above what they need. They go way beyond what they can afford. A good debt can become a bad debt when you overdo it.

2.   Investing in things that save us time or money and help us become much more efficient.
By doing these, we actually make more money. There are times when you have to put your money into expenses that will save you time, money, energy, and make you productive. One person's luxury is another person's utility and one person's utility is another person's luxury. You can't compare yourself with somebody else. What someone may be doing that you

consider as luxury may be utility to them. You have got to look at yourself to know where you are financially and know how much credit you can afford to improve your productivity in a way that will help you grow.

As you grow higher in your socioeconomic status, you realise that wealthy people don't use their money. They have mastered, instead, how to use other people's money to build wealth. If you invest in yourself by taking a relevant course or you borrow money to go to school or you do something to build yourself, that's good debt. At the end of the day, when you come out of that experience, you will be better off. You will be more exposed, and more productive. There are times you just have to invest in yourself even if it is beyond your means but it is good debt. Debt can be good if you are using it to acquire assets that are not depreciating; or if you are using it to build your own value.

Many of us need business loans to start a business. Don't say you want to save. Get investments and if you don't have investments, you can actually get a loan to finance your idea. That's some form of debt. It's a good way to invest and build up yourself. We must be smart about how we handle debt; we must not overdo it but engage it in a way that can build us up and help us build our own wealth.

The most familiar example of bad debt is credit cards. Credit cards have costly interest rates which compound quickly. It is only worth it if you pay off your balance at the end of the month. Credit card debts are the kinds of debts that have very high-interest rates and compound as the months go by. Credit cards have been designed to keep people in perpetual debt. The sad reality is that what many people put on credit cards are either assets that depreciate or things that don't improve their productivity. The credit card system has been designed in such a way as to lock you in the debt cycle, except you are sure your income can cover whatever the costs are. Credit cards are not evil; they are only problematic if you can't pay off your balance. If you can't pay off your balance all at once at the end of the month, it's ridiculous how much banks make from credit card debts. If you have credit card debts already, I advise you to enquire about making balance transfers with cheaper interest rates.

One of the good things about having a business in Australia is access to credit. With credit, you can improve your business productivity and protect yourself rather than taking money from your savings into your business. Let's assume I own a company that sells cups. I go to China to manufacture these cups and sell them elsewhere. If I want to scale up or get an order from a retailer like Woolworths to supply one million of these cups, where will I get the money? Of course, Woolworths will give me a down payment and will only pay the balance when the contract is fulfilled. To get capital for the contract, I may have to get credit or, better still, debt. I have to either go to a bank, get a loan, or seek investors to invest in my business. I have to raise capital. Rather than put my own money into it, I will raise capital from a bank to finance that project. I have been in conversations with Christian folks who don't understand how the world operates. When we don't understand how the world operates, our ability to sustain and create wealth will just be limited to salaries. A lot of people make billions of dollars from the stock market with other people's money.

Your approach to debt, whether it's good or bad, depends on you as an individual and your financial situation – what you can afford or not. Always make sure you live within your means but understand that the economy we live in is credit-driven. If you are deep in debt, cut your spending and stick to a budget. Put your debts on a payment plan and restructure your debts. There are a lot of debt management companies that can help you; they will consolidate your loans, reduce the interest, and review the terms. That way, you pay less in interest and you can get yourself back as soon as you can.

How Do I Raise Funds for a Startup?
You might seek seed investors depending on the field you are in but the mistake I see most people make is that their business is in their head. All they have is just an idea. Nobody will invest in what is in your head. You have to start something with your resources. Make the business concrete so that when you are making your presentation, people will believe in it and you will attract seed investors who are interested in early start-ups. You have got to be able to translate your idea into something verifiable. No investor will help you develop your prototype. You have got to have a working prototype and if it is a service, make sure you have the basic stuff in order.

You have got to have something that works and solves a problem. Don't run a business that does not solve a problem. Make sure the prototype, the service, or whatever you are doing solves a problem. People will be attracted to it when it solves a problem and is operational, even on a small scale.

8
NEGATIVE MINDSETS

The Mind

THE MIND IS LIKE the software that runs the hardware - the brain. The mind is a composite term that describes all the mental faculties of a person. All of the mental faculties of a person which include the ability to think, to feel, to emote, are captured in the mind. The mind is not tangible - it's not physical - but it is as real as anything else. Your mind is what makes you the person that you are. The mind and the brain are the connection point between the soul and body of a man.

We already understand that man by nature is a tripartite being. That is, man is a spirit that has a soul and lives in a body. Man is a spiritual being that has a soul. Our minds are actually part of our souls. So, that spirit-soul connection doesn't get separated in terms of our reality but your mind is a part of your soul. Your thinking, emotions, and will are encoded in your soul and then you live in a body.

Your mind controls your body through the brain. Your brain runs your mind. So often, when we talk about the heart, we refer to our core, our spirit. However, in the Bible, the heart is used interchangeably with the soul for the decision-making capability of a man. So when the Bible says, *'the heart of a man is desperately wicked'*, that scripture is not necessarily talking about the spirit, which is the breath God put in man. It is talking about the soul.

Two broad classifications of the mind are:
1. Conscious Mind
2. Subconscious Mind

Conscious Mind

This is that part of the mind you are aware of and can recognise. Starting from your sense of self-identity – knowing who you are, your personality, your thinking, your reasoning, and your decision-making. You decided to pick up this book to read it, that's your conscious mind at work. The part of the mind that encodes consciousness is housed in the neocortex, the outer part of the brain. It is also the most developed part of the brain where the conscious mind lies.

Parts of the conscious mind we should be aware of are:
- Thought - Thoughts are limitless. Your ability to think is encoded in your conscious mind. You have got to be conscious and alive for you to think.

- Imagination (Visual Thought) - Imaginations are also limitless. You can imagine things that have never existed. You can imagine things that happened before you were born. You can imagine Jesus even though you never met Him physically. You can imagine what will happen in the future even if it hasn't happened. You can imagine something so microscopic like an atom. You can imagine something so huge like the planetary bodies you have never been to. You can imagine life on Mars even though you may never step foot off this planet Earth. You can think about heaven, even though its glory is well beyond our imagination.

- Decision Making (Judgement) - The decisions we make all originate from the mind. Your ability to choose resides in your conscious mind.

- Intelligence and Creativity - Intelligence is different from creativity. Intelligence is your ability to reason and give an answer that is already predetermined. You are intelligent if you can produce a predetermined answer. Creativity is not about giving a predetermined answer to an existing problem. Creativity is about questioning the problem. Creativity is about finding the WHY behind the problem. Creativity is not about you giving us an answer. Creativity is about asking the right question. Creativity also seeks to provide solutions to problems that we did not know even existed. Creativity is the bedrock of innovation. This is why many creative people are not necessarily intelligent. As long as they can reason and generate solutions to problems that we didn't know existed, they are creative and all of these are encoded in the conscious mind.

- Personality - Your personality is an embodiment of your temperament, your training, your education, your life experiences, and your religious beliefs. All of those things come to form your personality. One key part of your personality is your temperament. Some of you must have read Tim LaHaye's book about the different temperaments but all of these are encoded in your personality and they are still part of the conscious mind, as well as attitude.

Subconscious Mind

Deeper down, there is another part of the brain that you are often not aware of - the subconscious mind. A lot of the behaviours, patterns, habits, impulses, and inclinations that we have originate from the subconscious mind. Conditioning originates from the subconscious mind. A lot of emotions are generated from the subconscious mind.

There is a lot more to the subconscious mind than the conscious mind. Many people think the mind is just for thinking, critical reasoning, and decision-making. Yes! Those are important for our day-to-day life as human beings. Someone said the greatest gift God gave man is free will. Your free will is exercised by your mind. You make decisions including pursuing a relationship with God through your mind. God does not deal with us below the level of our consciousness. So, when God relates with a man, he is fully conscious of God's dealings. You are aware that God is speaking to you, and you will often know that He is doing something in your life – even when the outcome is not immediately visible.

The reality is that there is a lot more to your subconscious mind than the conscious mind. The subconscious mind is connected to the limbic system, a part of the lower brain which is more primitive than the higher cognitive centres. Some of the functions of the limbic system are as follows :

- Stores non-conscious habits and behaviour patterns - The brain is a powerful predictive machine. The brain tries to predict future behaviour from past behaviour and this predictive ability starts in the subconscious – learning from the past. A lot of the impulses you have had started at the subconscious level because of your past experience.

- Regulates emotions - Emotions are biological programmes that run through your brain. They are natural and part of what makes you human. Your emotions are regulated by the subconscious mind. Your emotions are part of who you are. There is nothing like: *'Don't be emotional'* - everyone is emotional. You cannot separate your emotions from you. Your emotions are part of who you are. Emotions are part of your natural constitution. It is normal to feel emotions. The problem is that the emotions which are generated by a small, tiny structure, called the amygdala, can spread to the cortex or upper part of the brain. There, the brain gives it meaning and it develops into feelings. When you overlay feelings with an experience that is positive, you can get bonding and attachment. But when you overlay the feelings with negative experiences, you may get anxiety.

• Forms and stores memory - Memories of events, people, places, and so on are formed by and stored in our subconscious minds. This is one of the reasons why the subconscious mind is very powerful.

• Involved in navigation and intuition - There is a lot more that happens in your subconscious mind than in your conscious mind. Your conscious mind is just the tip of the iceberg. There is a lot more to your mind, your habits, your emotion, and all of these things happen in your subconscious.

The issue I find is that so many people get the concept of mind wrong. They don't understand the scope of their minds. When the Bible says, '*And be not conformed to this world: but be ye transformed by the renewing of your mind...'* (Romans 12:2 KJV), the Bible is not just referring to your conscious mind which is your decision-making capability but to your subconscious mind. Your job, as a leader, is to understand how your mind works and how you can get your mind renewed appropriately, particularly your subconscious mind. I see over and over again that a lot of people will never rise to their potential because of their belief systems, not because of what happens or their circumstances.

Someone said life is 1% what happens to you and 99% how you react to it. There is more to life in your reactions than your actions. So your belief system, your conditioning, your habits, and your emotions, are all very important. If you don't understand how they work, how you are wired, and how you improve your productivity by working on your mind and getting your mind in the best possible shape, you will always struggle.

The brain learns by experience. Every sensory experience goes through a process termed by psychologists as value tagging. Our brain attaches value to every new experience based on our experience or past knowledge. This is why we get certain vibes from people we don't know - our brains try to value the encounter based on our experience with people with similar traits. As a result, certain things are triggered within us before that person even opens their mouth.

The brain doesn't always get it right because many times, God will bring opportunities that we will judge as not good enough and your brain will make you put your walls up and not recognise what God is doing at that point in time. This is because your brain will always rely on the past. When Jesus came, the Jews did not recognise Him because in their minds they thought the Messiah would physically defeat Rome, so they doubted Jesus and did not take Him seriously and that is why their attitude towards Him was negative. Many times, our belief systems and our attitudes are already predetermined because of the state of our subconscious. A lot of people do not have healthy self-esteem because they have always been told that they couldn't really do anything well, so that became their default conditioning.

God doesn't work that way. There are many times that God will give us a word or an instruction to do things that are outside our previous experience; our brain cannot relate to it or unravel it and because our brains have been trained to always go back to our previous experience, we miss it. Most people who have been conditioned to react in a particular way are not even aware of the conditioning that has taken place in their minds.

Subconscious Processes

- Selective Attention

Your brain cannot cope with all the information you are exposed to. What the brain does is that it directs the focus of your reality to the sensations that matter. Multitasking is biologically impossible. Every time you think you are multitasking, you are actually task-switching. However, this happens so fast (within microseconds) that you wouldn't even know. Your brain selects what is important and your brain will direct your focus to what is important.

Selective attention is your brain's ability to direct its focus to what is really important. This is important because you cannot be fully productive if you cannot control your focus. A problem that limits a lot of people's productivity is a problem of focus. One of the reasons why you cannot be a master in what you have been called to do is a lack of selective attention.

- Value Tagging

Every experience you have, your brain puts a tag on it. Certain things happen to you or you meet certain people and you attach a negative value to them and nothing can be done for you to see them in a better light. It starts from the subconscious mind. If you are unable to attach the proper value to an experience or a person, if you always judge the book by the cover, you will miss a lot of God-orchestrated opportunities. Do not tag the wrong value to the right experience based on your previous experience.

- Learned Helplessness

Exposure to uncontrollable outcomes will over a period of time lead to a degradation in your decision-making ability. Why is it that people who fail just keep failing and failing? That is learned helplessness. Learned helplessness is one of the reasons why addicts find it very hard to break away from their bad habits. Learned helplessness is one of the subconscious principles of human behaviour. Every defeat you suffer sets you up for another defeat until you break the cycle of learned helplessness.

'Whatever we plant in our subconscious mind and nourish with repetition and emotion will one day become a reality' – Earl Nightingale

You can fix your subconscious by:
- Raising subconscious desires, biases and priorities into your conscious mind.
- Intentionally focus on goals and plans.

Experience Changes the Brain

No matter how you are wired or how conditioned your mind is, your mind can be renewed. The brain is always in a constant state of change, so experience can change your brain.

Rewiring Your Brain

Your subconscious mind is the gatekeeper to your attention. For those suffering from an addiction, who keep stumbling over the same stone, it's time to break the cycle of helplessness. This chapter of the book is designed to walk you through this journey of getting free so that you can liberate your mind and accept what God has prepared for you.

If you allow your mind to go everywhere or let your untrained and unrefined mind decide for you, you will make mistakes because your mind will always go to the past. Your mind will go to what society has decided is good for you. Your life is a daily choice. Every day of your life, you are making choices and what most of us don't understand is that our subconscious mind controls our choices.

Neuroplasticity

Neuroplasticity is derived from two words, *neuro* which means the brain or the mind, and *plasticity* which is gotten from plastic and means flexible, or something that can be twisted, bent, or changed. Many of us believe our brains and minds are fixed. '*This is the way I am*' is a popular cause of argument between couples. The reality is that people change; their brains or minds can change. The popular idea is that after the age of 21, your brain is set and can't change. This is not true - the brain can change. The brain is flexible and plastic in its own way.

We already know that the brain develops significantly from the age of 0 to 21 in different ways. New brain cells are formed every time a child has a new experience. The established networks in the brain become more robust. Neuroplasticity occurs in the brains of children, adolescents, teenagers, and young adults. Most people believe that by the age of 18, the brain is fully formed, which is why most countries have the age of 18 as the mark of maturity. If someone commits a crime before the age of 18, they will be treated and tried as minors. They might still go to jail but only as a juvenile. But after the age of 18, they are treated as full-grown adults. Now, we know that the brain continues to develop even after the age of 65. The brain has the inherent ability to keep developing.

Neuroplasticity is vital because it helps the brain to keep adapting to change. So, if you want to learn a new skill, start a new project, form a new habit, reinforce something that you are already doing in a deeper way, or become an expert at something you are average at right now, then you will need to stretch your brain. When you want to form a new habit and apply yourself with commitment, you are changing your brain. You are enhancing neuroplasticity. If you are going to be an effective leader, you have to bring in this principle.

Factors that enhance neuroplasticity are:
- Environment

- Experience
- Effort

Environment

Your environment plays a crucial role in neuroplasticity because your brain is an expert organ in getting information from your environment. Your brain is exposed to so many sensory impulses all the time. To a large extent, the performance of your brain or mind depends on the environment you are exposed to. If you grow up bilingual or multilingual, once you stop using or speaking one of the languages, you will lose it because the representation of those languages in the brain starts to shrink.

If you are going to expand your leadership ability in whatever area; whether in self-leadership, thought leadership, or whatever area, you have got to put yourself in an environment where you are surrounded by people who feel what you feel, and who are passionate about what you are passionate about. If you have a call to teenagers, for instance, you have got to be in groups of people who feel the same thing you feel. If you don't do it, you will be frustrated. Your environment matters a lot. If there is anything you need to start taking an audit of, it is your environment. The top five people you spend time with will determine to a large extent the kind of person you will turn out to be. Our brains and minds are shaped by our environments.

I am not saying don't expose your mind to various ideas. As a leader, you should be broad and open-minded. We can't affect our world when we are not open-minded and broad in our thinking. Exposure is key in leadership but you have to be very careful of the kind of things that you expose your mind to – the books you read, the people that you allow to influence you – because this is a subconscious process. When you are under the influence of someone and you see them over and over again, at a subconscious level plasticity starts to take place in the brain and the mind that you may start to imitate them without knowing. You must make sure you control and intentionally choose the kind of experience that you find yourself in. Your environment, to a large extent, controls the experiences that you have. The kind of environment you allow your mind to be exposed to determines the kind of experience that you have.

Effort

I was in London for my 10th wedding anniversary and I was driven around by the Black Cab Drivers in London. One of the things that struck me was that these guys knew all the routes. Most of them didn't need to consult Google Maps or anything like that. After that trip, I read about Black Cab drivers and saw research about a special test these drivers take - which can take a minimum of nine months. The study was done on 79 Black Cab drivers. After going through the learning phase, the researchers found a significant increase in the size of the hippocampus, and their memory capacity increased significantly. That tells you that memory capacity can be improved through a lot of effort. Some of the drivers were migrants who had gone through a lot of stuff. Some were old, and some were changing jobs. The research showed that any time you put effort into learning a new skill, you expand or stretch the capacity of your memory to develop those skills. So as a leader, if you are going to stretch your mind for self-government and everything else you want to do, you will need to put in intense effort.

Emotion

In a study of first-time fathers, what they realised is that the hormonal profile of a man who has just become a father is sort of skewed. First-time fathers tend to have a high level of testosterone, which is the hormone for sexual drive. But when they start to hold their children and bond with their children, they start to produce oxytocin, which is the hormone for bonding and it comes with contact. Fathers that were having contact with their children were having more oxytocin and were having more empathy and were more attached. Emotions also play a huge part in neuroplasticity.

Counterclockwise Experiment
This experiment was done in the United States. They got three different groups of people in their eighties. Those in Group 1 were told to live normally for one week. So, if you were in a group home, you stay in a group home, if you were in your own home, you stay in your own home. Group 2 members were given tasks that would cause them to reminisce on what it felt like living in their sixties for one week. Every activity they did for that one week will remind them of what life was about 20 years ago. Group 3 members were taken to retrofitted homes that looked like their homes 20 years ago. So, they did not ask them to reflect on the past, they created a place that looked exactly like where they were living 20 years ago which just

brought back memories for them. If you were not using a walking stick 20 years ago, it was taken away. Those that were not using glasses then had their glasses taken away. Everything they were not using 20 years ago was taken away. When they took them to the house, they didn't even help them carry their bag. They just dropped them in front of the house and left. When they came back in one week, the people in group 3 showed significant improvement in their visual acuity and musculoskeletal condition.

Taking them to the home they were living in 20 years earlier, just being in that environment, stimulated their brains and stretched their capacities so much that just by going up the stairs back and forth and finding a way to not lean on a walking stick, they actually improved. The people in Group 2 also showed improvement compared to Group 1. That tells us about the brain and the mind's ability to adapt to the environment.

The kind of effort that yields results involve:
- Practice - Once you know what you have been called to do, practice it.
- Repetition - Repeat it over and over again.
- Goal-directed - Whatever thing you are doing, let it be directed towards a goal.

The best way to master a skill is by practicing it. I know you must have heard about that before, so I want to tell you that there is a neuroscientific mechanism behind this called myelination. The nerves in the brain are surrounded by a coat of myelin which is an insulation that makes the nerve conduct faster. When you practice over and over again even if it is a skill you already have and you keep practicing over and over again, what you are doing is that you are myelinating those fibres, you are strengthening the nervous connections in your brain, and by doing that you become good at it. The mechanism by which you improve an already acquired skill is called myelination. Myelination takes you to that expert level.

If you are going to develop a brand-new skill that you didn't have before, your brain will have to form new brain cells (neurogenesis). This is acquired through goal-directed efforts with practice and repetition. There are 3 things that can help you enhance the process of neurogenesis. They are:

1. New experiences

When you expose yourself to new experiences, you stretch your mind. Always keep exploring new things in the area where God has called you. Never be satisfied. New experiences help to develop the brain more. Our brain thrives on novelty. Meet new people, and read other people's books.

2. Emotionally Intense Experiences

When emotions are involved in our experiences, they stick. If you want to develop something new, be passionate about it. When God gives you a vision, it might be bigger than you but even if it is bigger than you, be passionate about it. Don't be lifeless and mechanical in your approach to whatever you are doing. Whatever you are doing that is making a difference, be passionate about it. If you are not putting in your energy, or your effort, and you are not being deliberate, it will not work.

How do you create sustainable change in the brain?
- Raised awareness
- Focused attention
- Deliberate action
- Accountability

Raised Awareness

This speaks about the ability to bring non-conscious thoughts to the conscious. Things that you do that come from that sense of raised awareness are the ones that last. Behaviour change can only be sustainable if it is preceded by raised awareness. You have to dig deep, find your purpose, and move it from being unconscious to the point of consciousness where you know it, and it is as real to you as anything else. That awareness often comes when you are at the lowest of your lows. There has got to be a purpose behind that new behavioural change, idea, and project, and you must have clarity about it. You have to dig deep and find your why; it will come up to you because it will consume you.

Focused Attention

Once you are aware of your WHY, the next step is to focus your attention on that thing. Olakunle Soriyan said, *'Attention is the most in demand quality and it will be in the next 10, 20 years'*. Everybody is vying for your attention, every brand is vying for your attention because our attention is the most significant part of our cognition that directs our focus. Your attention directs your activities, and your life.

You must find a way to channel your attention to what you become aware of; you need to find a way to direct the focus of your attention to where God has called you to. You can't be everywhere. Even if you are multitalented, you have a dominant gift that should be a priority. You don't have to say YES to everybody. One of the things you must learn, as a leader is how to say NO. Saying no is a skill that if you lack, will make you miss your dreams.

Deliberate Action

This involves practice, repetition, and goal-directedness. You have to be deliberate about every one of those steps. You have to deliberately choose the actions that you focus your attention on.

Accountability

You have to be accountable to yourself, which involves journaling and self-reflection. Journaling is a really important habit to develop. Journaling simply involves sitting down to reflect and write your thoughts on how you see different things. Having a gratitude journal is really helpful. You have to set reminders. To foster better accountability, you can have a partner or a coach, a mentor, or someone to hold you accountable.

9

BUILDING HEALTHY RELATIONSHIPS

≈≈≈

THERE IS NO WAY around the fact that we have got to deal with other people. God has created us as relational beings. Relationships define us. God designed us to have a horizontal relationship with people around us – in our world and sphere of influence (family, neighbours, colleagues, etc.) – as well as people outside our sphere of influence. Also, God expects us to have a vertical relationship with Him. He is the God of relationships. God is love personified. Love is not love if it is not shared. Love gives and cares. God wants to show His love to others, that's why He created us to be objects of His love. When God says you should love your neighbour as yourself, it is because He is laying a demand on that seed of love that is already on your inside. Love is like a stream that flows from the top of the mountain. It can't be stopped; it must flow down.

Love flows from your heart! If you have it, it has to flow. We are always in contact with people, hence always needing to show love.

Relationships can affect our quality of life. We enjoy our lives better when our relationships work and are healthy. When our relationships are broken, life becomes more stressful. This happens when there is a heartbreak or relationships are strained which causes stress. '*Can two walk together unless they are agreed*'? (Amos 3:3 NKJV) Two people can only co-exist if they agree.

So, what are the key elements that will help us get along with other people? We see that in Matthew 5:9 (NKJV) which says, '*Blessed are the peacemakers for they shall be called the sons of God*' That word peacemakers is taken from the Greek word *eirenopoios*. *Eiren* means peace while *poios* means to make or to do. Therefore, a peacemaker is someone that makes peace. It is someone that cultivates peace. It's an action word. Peacemakers actively cultivate an atmosphere of peace and tranquility. They don't want strife, arguments, or dissension. It doesn't mean there can't be misunderstandings but they seek peace. A peacemaker is constantly interested in building bridges in relationships.

Proverbs 17:14 says, *'The beginning of strife is like releasing water, therefore stop contention before a quarrel starts'* Imagine two people fighting in a muddy pool that is messy but what started that muddy pool was a tap that was left open to run. The best way to stop a muddy pool from developing is by turning off a tap. This is what a peacemaker does. There are times we want to release the pressure in our tanks. These are pressures that can come from disagreements, quarrels, dislike, etc. When we allow this water to run from our tanks uncontrolled, we create a muddy pool that can become a trip hazard. If you want to learn to get along with others, you must learn to turn off the tap. People will always bring attitudes that will build up pressure in us to turn our taps open but if we learn to resist that temptation, we avoid a lot of quarrels.

When our words and actions are peaceful, we will find that our relationships will be wholesome and healthy. That doesn't mean we won't have disagreements or different views, those will happen but there are ways of controlling those negative energies without releasing the tap or flooding the whole yard.

God wants us to avoid strife. Strife is that state of contention, contest, and quarrel that is intense and not beneficial. You can have a respectful disagreement with someone where both parties are able to settle things amicably. That's not strife. When disagreements become heated such that both parties hurt each other or it degenerates to malice, then that is strife at work. When you allow strife to enter into a relationship, it leads to all kinds of problems and those types of relationships never last. Relationships require maintenance. If we will get along with people, a lot of work is required. *'Let nothing be done through selfish ambition or conceit but in lowliness of mind, let each esteem others better than himself'* (Philippians 2:3 NKJV)

Every single person on earth has some form of flaw. No one is altogether perfect. Also, no one on earth knows everything. You may be an expert or genius in a field but nobody has a monopoly of knowledge. This should make you lowly in mind. It should make you conclude that there is a lot you need to learn. Listen, the best car has not been built, the best genius has not been born, the best inventor has not even opened a workshop, the best educator has not started teaching, etc. The best is yet to come. It doesn't matter what you have achieved. Even if you have set a record in a particular sport or activity, that record can be broken because it becomes the motivation of other people. This realisation should make you lowly, not timid, or having a sense of low self-esteem. It should only make you humble and unselfish.

One of the challenges with this generation is that we are so self-absorbed or selfish, and we have got to be very careful. We should stop thinking only about ourselves and how we can get what we want even when it means breaking laws or bending rules just to satisfy our desires. This cannot help if you are going to get along with people. You've got to be humble if you must get along with people. No matter the position you are holding generally, there is a lot you can learn from others around you, it doesn't matter even if you are the boss. You don't know everything. There is something you can learn from others.

'Likewise you younger people, submit yourselves to your elders. Yes, all of you be submissive to one another, and be clothed with humility, for "God resists the proud, But gives grace to the humble."' (1 Peter 5:5 NKJV) As a young

person, submitting here doesn't mean you lose your sense of agency and identity. It just means you allow them to go first and then engage them respectfully. However, the elders are also meant to submit to the younger people because nobody has a monopoly of knowledge. We must all be clothed in humility. Grace only comes to the humble. A proud person will not desire grace. No help comes the way of the proud. When you acknowledge that you need grace, God will use relationships around you to fill the gaps. When you see relationships around you as if you are better, more dignified, more privileged, etc. than them, then you cannot receive anything from them because you have minimised them.

Saul did not see how David could kill Goliath until he started reeling out his CV about how he had killed the lion and bear with the help of God. David was so sure that Goliath will die just like the lion and the bear. Saul finally agreed and asked David to go with his armour. However, David refused it because it was too heavy and he decided to do it his way. Saul saw value in David, so he allowed him to go ahead to fight Goliath. There is value in the seemingly insignificant relationships around you. As a parent, you can get value from your children. If my attitude to my son is that he is too young and can't do anything significant, then I won't be able to influence him in any significant way. Our attitude must always be positive.

We must also be willing to serve other people if we want to get along well with people. Relationships grow in the atmosphere of humility and service (not servitude). We must learn to help other people by showing care and giving assistance. We must be concerned about other people's welfare. This is what fuels relationships.

How to Build up a Good Relationship

1. **Treat people the way you want to be treated**: *'Therefore, whatever you want men to do to you, do also to them, for this is the Law and the Prophets'* (Matthew 7:12) You must learn to treat other people the way you want to be treated. If you want people to respect you, treat them with respect. If you want people to listen to you, listen to them. If you want others to welcome you, you must be welcoming too.

2. **Use pleasant words**: *'Pleasant words are like a honeycomb, Sweetness to the soul and health to the bones'* (Proverbs 16:24). To build a wholesome

relationship, you have got to master using pleasant words - words that build up and encourage. Even when the person is low or disappointing, pleasant words can build them up. Pleasant words create an atmosphere for growth and change. If good words can build a relationship, bad words can also tear down a relationship. The tongue can be a blessing and a curse at the same time if not properly managed. (James 3:5-10) There is a tendency for our tongues to release hurtful words to people. This is why we need the help of the Holy Spirit.

3. **Forgiveness**: *'He who covers a transgression seeks love, But he who repeats a matter separates friends'.* (Proverbs 17:9). It's important to be quick to forgive people when they wrong us. It doesn't mean we just sweep issues under the carpet as it is necessary to confront issues, however, in love. After this has been done, then the wrong should be covered in forgiveness. That's how to sustain friendship relationships. We move on after we have settled a matter. To keep bringing up matters that have been settled is to break a friendship.

4. **Gentleness**: *'Let your gentleness be known to all men. The Lord is at hand'*. (Philippians 4:5). The Lord expects us to be gentle and mild towards other people; not rash or explosive. If you have an explosive personality, you need to seek God's help. Our words and actions must point people to Jesus in us.

Dealing with Difficult People

Have you had any difficult people in your life? Have you met someone you just couldn't get along with? Have you been in a situation where you need someone and can't get rid of them but you are just not connecting with that person? I have been in that situation. During my specialist training, there was this man who was my boss. Initially, when he chose me for the job, he was keen on me. I came in from Newcastle at the time to Sydney and went to some hospitals and that was not my first choice but he called me and said he had seen my CV and my profile, so he wanted me. We started well, but along the line, I discovered it was difficult to get along well. It was always one issue or the other. He was very hard to please, and it was very difficult to get his approval. He would rebuke me in the presence of a patient without any regard. It was a struggle and I started to doubt myself. I started to feel I wasn't good enough. I felt I couldn't cope in this specialty. I was taking presentations every week and it was very draining because he was always at the front interrupting me. I started to get very nervous about presentations. It was just pressure upon pressure. Of course, I could not talk back because I needed his signature to sign off that year.

I understood that this man was in my life for a reason and I decided to change my attitude towards the middle of the year. I decided to start attending his clinics and by the end of the year, I discovered that I began to operate at a high level of proficiency. In fact, I had almost finished in my first year the requirement of three years. It was later, in retrospect, that I realised that although this man made my life difficult – because he was borderline racist and I later discovered after I had left the hospital that he had bipolar disorder, he was divorced, and his life was a mess – he was in my life for a reason. I learnt a lot of neurophysiology from him and that is what I do now.

About two years ago during my Ph.D. studies, I was presenting a paper at the International Conference

Centre in Sydney and he was there in the audience. I presented novel research. We were colleagues because we now work in the same core specialty and he didn't remember what he made me go through at that time. We just had a very good discussion afterward.

God allows some people into our lives not because He wants to crush us or rob us of our self-confidence but because He wants to build us up. The problem most times is that we don't know how to handle those kinds of people in our lives. Everyone reading this will find somebody in their life who will stretch them or challenge them.

God wants us to strive for peace at all times no matter what. God's demand on us is to strive for peace (Hebrews 12:14). God wants us to pursue peace with all men as much as possible. In Romans 12:18, the Bible states clearly that if it is possible, we should pursue peace with all men. All men include people that believe in you, people that doubt you, naturally difficult people, and all kinds of people. When we talk about difficult people, we are not only talking about angry people. Some difficult people are just too cold towards you - you find it very hard to get a reaction from them.

The Bible says whether they are warm towards you and affectionate towards you or cold and repulsive, follow peace with all men. That is the central motive when it comes to dealing with people.

The other very important thing that we must do when dealing with difficult people is in Philippians 2:3, *'Let nothing be done through selfish ambition or conceit, but in lowliness of mind let each esteem others better than himself'* (NKJV). One important characteristic that we need in dealing with difficult people is dealing with people generally with lowliness of mind and not arrogance or an egotistical approach. James 3:17 says *'But the wisdom that is from above is first pure, then peaceable, gentle, willing to yield, full of mercy and good fruits, without partiality and without hypocrisy'*. When God gives you the wisdom to deal with a difficult person, that wisdom will promote peace, it will help you do something that is pure, not sinful, and it will help you pursue peace as much as possible. That wisdom will make you gentle. When someone is gentle, they don't offend people and when you are meek you don't get easily offended.

These are principles that we have to work with if we are going to deal with difficult people - the principle of pursuing peace with all men irrespective of how they treat you and the principle of humility and avoiding self-propagation. These are principles that cut across every situation and area of life.

How Do You Handle a Boss or Someone Who Always Picks on You

We may not be able to control how a lot of people treat us but we can control how we react. We can control what our disposition will be toward those people. You can still respond but when you respond and you are calmer, your response is much more analytical and much less emotional. When you are too emotionally charged, a lot of your actions will bypass your cortex, which is your thinking brain and a lot of your actions will be based on your feeling brain.

A good example is people who have gone through a traumatic break-up and any of those parties rushes into another relationship without healing from the first. The result is that their emotions will be charged and they will not be making rational decisions, so they end up hurting themselves more. But when you relax and your emotions are calm, you can respond in a way that will not hurt you or bring blame back to you.

Most people are trying to get a reaction out of us. Most times, those reactions are not precise because there are too many emotions involved, so you may bring too many references that are not relevant or you may go to a place that you don't want to go to. Having a conversation is a targeted response, not a reaction. That will be most effective.

Maybe we are difficult sometimes. Everyone has a streak of difficulty in them. We all have at some point been difficult people. With patience and intentionality, we get to understand that people are going through things that they then project to other people. Showing love to difficult people actually works. There are times when we are in our low moments and we give it back to other people. Some of the people we think are difficult – if only we see them from a different side, with prayer and understanding – are people we may actually be able to get on our side and experience a different angle to them.

As a believer, walking in the spirit is non-negotiable. When your expiry date has come in a place, God will make the place difficult for you but there are also times when there are Canaanites in your Promised Land that you have to flush out. You, by the Spirit of God, would know what is happening. There are times when you know it's time for you to move, you just feel it. It could be in a church where there is no growth, no passion, going to church is not enjoyable, you are not learning - it's either you are fighting with someone or someone is criticising you. You are not growing and you are getting bitter. God might just want you to move on. A good example of this at work is David running away from Saul. If David had stayed with Saul, he would have died with Saul and never become king. There are times when you have to leave the palace because there is a Saul there and that Saul is carrying a judgement.

There are other times that the devil will raise people to make you feel this is not where you should be, so you move away amiss. In those situations, you have to discern, go into that spiritual battle and pray. Be wise and careful about the way you go ahead with things. Walking in the spirit and having an understanding is really key.

How Do You Deal with Someone Who Always Has to be Right about Everything or Always Wants to Have Their Way

'If anyone forces you to go one mile, go with them two miles'
(Matthew 5:41 NIV)

When we are confronted by difficult people who want to have their way, we should show wisdom instead of weakness and sometimes wisdom helps us yield to others. When Abraham and his nephew, Lot, had to separate and pick between two different lands, Abraham let Lot choose first when it should have been the other way around. Abraham was not being weak, rather he was wise because he knew the covenant he had with God. There are times when we have to let peace reign and deal with wisdom. Lose the battle without losing the war. We must pick our battles right and as we rely on the Holy Spirit, God will help us.

Yielding to other people does not necessarily mean weakness, it also doesn't mean being treated poorly by the other person. You find the right way, the right moment to express yourself without crossing any boundaries, without hurting other people. Make sure your motive for talking is not to hurt the other person also but to bring their attention to the hurt they are causing you and the pain you are experiencing so they can be sensitive to you as well. You do that in a way that is amicable, sensible, and at the end of the day, you are pursuing peace. If your emotions get the best of you, quickly try to fix them.

We must be able to freely express ourselves and allow other people to contribute. Make sure your goal is to advocate for yourself, speak for yourself, and don't let anyone take you for a ride. People who naturally do that are not excessive in their reaction and they don't cross any boundaries. Don't do anything that would come across as offensive or verbally abusive. Don't speak when your emotions are high. Don't let your emotions cloud your judgement. If you are trying to correct people or report people when you are emotional, you will be the one at fault. You can't separate your emotions from you but just chill a little bit and say it in a very controlled way.

Walk In Love

Our attitude to those who mistreat us should be that of love. We are children of God. How we treat others should be the way God treats them, not the way they treat us.

[43] You have heard that it was said, 'You shall love your neighbor and hate your enemy.' [44] But I say to you, love your enemies, bless those who curse you, do good to those who hate you, and pray for those who spitefully use you and persecute you, [45] that you may be sons of your Father in heaven; for He makes His sun rise on the evil and on the good, and sends rain on the just and on the unjust. [46] For if you love those who love you, what reward have you? Do not even the tax collectors do the same? [47] And if you greet your brethren only, what do you do more than others? Do not even the tax collectors do so? [48] Therefore you shall be perfect, just as your Father in heaven is perfect. (Matthew 5:43-48 NKJV)

If we love only those who love us, then we are not any better. God expects us to love those who don't deserve it. We are not meant to love only those who get along well with us. There will always be difficult people around us, and we are expected to still deal with them in love.

¹⁴ Bless those who persecute you; bless and do not curse. ¹⁵ Rejoice with those who rejoice, and weep with those who weep. ¹⁶ Be of the same mind toward one another. Do not set your mind on high things, but associate with the humble. Do not be wise in your own opinion. ¹⁷ Repay no one evil for evil. Have regard for good things in the sight of all men. ¹⁸ If it is possible, as much as depends on you, live peaceably with all men. ¹⁹ Beloved, do not avenge yourselves, but rather give place to wrath; for it is written, "Vengeance is Mine, I will repay," says the Lord. ²⁰ Therefore "If your enemy is hungry, feed him; If he is thirsty, give him a drink; For in so doing you will heap coals of fire on his head." ²¹ Do not be overcome by evil, but overcome evil with good. (Romans 12:14-21 NKJV)

The standard of God for us has not changed, we are meant to bless those who curse us. We are not expected to pay evil for evil. We are not expected to be overcome by evil but to overcome evil with good. Revenge should not be in our vocabulary. Vengeance belongs to God. What we owe every man (difficult or not) is love. Love must be our watchword. Love must dictate our actions. And whether people deserve it or not, we must still give it!

10
EXCEEDING EXPECTATIONS

≈≈≈

'For surely there is an end; And thine expectation shall not be cut off.
Proverbs 23:18 KJV

'For surely there is a hereafter, And your hope will not be cut off
Proverbs 23:18 NKJV

IF YOUR SON TELLS you that he wants to go play basketball and you say, 'You will not', does that give room for negotiation? There is no negotiation, that's case closed. If you don't do that to your kids, they will take advantage of you. So scriptures say that 'your expectation will not be cut short'. That is a statement of authority. That is a statement of certainty, that is a statement that is loaded. It connotes finality. You will not! Your expectation will not be cut short. Surely there is an end and your expectation will not be cut short. There is a future for you and that future is glorious. The Bible says in Jeremiah 29:11, *'For I know the thoughts that I think toward you, saith the LORD, thoughts of peace, and not of evil, to give you an expected end'*. Surely God has great plans for you. Surely there is a future and that future is a beautiful, glorious future and it says that your expectation of that future will not be cut short.

We are going a step further, we are talking about exceeding expectations. The New Living Translation of Proverbs 23:18 says *'…. Your hope will not be disappointed'*. I prophesy over your life that your expectation will be exceeded, in Jesus' name. The word 'expectation' in Proverbs 23:18 is taken from the Hebrew word *tiqvâh* which means a cord, an attachment. A good example of a cord is the umbilical cord which mothers are very conversant with. The umbilical cord attaches the mother to the fetus. The word expectation means a cord or an attachment. Your expectation is a cord that attaches you to your desired future. That property, that running theme that God has given you, etc., your expectation is the cord that attaches you to your desired future. When He says your expectation will not be cut short, that word in

Proverbs 23:18 is picturing a cord and He says it will not be cut because the connection between you and the future God has for you is that cord and as long as you are connected to that future through that cord, you are going to get there. That cord – that attachment that connects you to your miracle, that connects you to what God has in store for you – is your expectation and it is going to deliver. Your expectation will come to pass as long as it is attached. As long as you are connected, your expectations will come to pass. There may be a delay or you may wander for a long time.

God gave Abraham the word that he will be a father of nations. There was an expectation but there was also a delay. Some of you are labouring right now and you are not seeing the signs, you are working hard but you are not seeing the sign. You have planted your bamboo for ten years, fifteen years and not one single shoot of the blade has emerged and you are like *'Is it still there? Is there still seed here'?* Let me tell you this, when it shoots up, it will go beyond six meters within six weeks. Some of you are in what we call *'The Valley of Latent Disappointment'*. You have been to the gym for six months and you have not lost one kilo. Then tomorrow you have another gym session and you are like, *'Oh My God'*! and you check your credit card account and they have removed $10 again this week. That's The Valley of Latent Disappointment - you are not seeing the signs but you are putting in the effort. Your expectation, as long as you are in the right place and you are connected, will deliver. It will deliver. I want you to be encouraged today that what God has told you concerning your life, career, business, family, parents, children, etc. will happen. It will deliver! You may have been knocked down, you may have been knocked back, you may have been knocked away but it is time for you to enter through the door.

An expectation is a strong belief about a desired future. Nobody will deliver your future to you. You will deliver your future because your expectation is what really counts. I am encouraging you, my brother, don't give up on that dream. I am encouraging you, my sister, there is still hope. *'For there is hope of a tree, if it be cut down, that it will sprout again, and that the tender branch thereof will not cease. Though the root thereof wax old in the earth, and the stock thereof die in the ground; Yet through the scent of water it will bud, and bring forth boughs like a plant'* (Job 14:7-9 KJV). You will rise again. I want to encourage you to stand on the Word of God. *'For blessed is she that believed: for there shall be a performance of those things which were told her from the Lord'* (Luke

1:45 KJV). I am telling you the truth, there shall be a performance. You may not see the signs, your bank account may be empty right now. You may be debt-ridden and not even sure where you will go but there shall be a performance. God will not start something that He will not complete. He will not send you on a journey that He has not provided for. You are sourced already for your destiny.

How Do We Get Expectations?

When you expect something, it involves the faculties of your mind. Expectations can come from two sources. You get expectations from experience and you can get expectations from instructions. Sometimes, we develop expectations through our experiences. If you have more than one child, for instance, when the second child came, you already had the experience so you had some expectations about when the child will start to smile, sit, crawl, and all of those things because you have had an experience. Experience sometimes creates expectations for the future. A mother who has had a child before – when talking to people who are about to have a child – can help build those expectations based on her experience. So, our experience determines the kind of expectations we have. Have you met someone who is doing the kind of job you want to do and when you go to their house, you are like, 'I wish for this' and if you have the opportunity of being in their role, you are expecting to manifest what they manifest because of your experience.

Expectations can also come from instructions. Meaning you might not have experienced it but you can be instructed about it. A lot of new migrants to a new country may not have experienced the country before but they have been told or instructed about the country, so they build expectations based on what they have been told. Guess what? Sometimes those expectations go off. I watched a video about Australia in 2007, a 1-hour infomercial on BBC Radio sponsored by the Government and they showed all these doctors from India and Bangladesh. I love Australia. It's a beautiful country. I have been here for four years. I can't forget the image of this doctor in a boat fishing with his family. He said, *'We have been here for four years and we are citizens of the country. I am a surgeon'*. That was the first time Australia came on my radar. Guess what? I landed here with the expectation of taking over. I thought Australia needed doctors but I didn't even ask myself what kind of doctors they needed. The doctor with an Indian accent on the infomercial, do I know if he has practiced in the U.K for the last ten years? He has got kids that are teenagers. Has he been practicing for 15 years?

I came here post-graduation, fresh from Medical School in a third-world country where all I knew were tuberculosis, HIV, and malaria. Almost half of our patients had typhoid. I had never interpreted an MRI before. We didn't even have an MRI Scan in our hospital. I got here with expectations but very quickly I started to adjust my CV after passing the exams and I realised that as a doctor I was unemployable. Then I started applying for Physiotherapy, I didn't even know that as a doctor I needed a degree in Physiotherapy. I started applying to be a cleaner in the local hospital. I applied to be a cleaner and that was within three months because I was desperate. I applied for a blood collector and they rejected me - an intern and an expert. I wouldn't even need to look at you twice, I knew where the vein was. Like all those professional darts, I will throw my cannula and it will enter the vein. Then I applied for a job as a phlebotomist and they said, 'Sorry' Sorry? With an MBBS.? We took care of HIV patients without gloves. I am telling you the truth. I was rejected and my expectation did not come to pass.

I cried in my room and to make matters worse, I didn't have money. $500 finished within a week. I thought $500 was money until I bought food in Johannesburg, South Africa, about $35 for lunch. I had queued for about 20 minutes, so when it got to my turn, I couldn't talk. The food was $35 and there was a very long queue. I had to buy it by force. That $35 when converted to my local currency was about 2 weeks' wage. Just for one meal! I didn't eat until I landed in Australia. I was determined not to spend another dollar. My expectation was remarkably dashed based on my instruction. Based on what I was hoping for. Sometimes, our expectations are based on our experience and expectations.

'Now unto him that is able to do exceeding abundantly above all that we ask or think, according to the power that worketh in us' (Ephesians 3:20 KJV).

The other day, I was watching a football match of the World Cup. It was Iran against Wales and these guys kept fighting and fighting. They scored two goals in the injury time of the game. I was just thinking that if in injury time, these people could still be persistent against all odds, how much more waiting on God? There is nothing God has shown you that He will not deliver. He will not show you a dream that He will not help you fulfill. He will not plant a desire in your heart without the means of fulfillment. He will not give you a wife that He will not give you the resources to look after. God will not help you start a journey that you will not fulfill. It may be challenging and some of you may have to hope against hope, you know what that means? When all hope is lost but you are still hoping. Why are you hoping? You are not hoping based on your strength but because there is somebody who is able. God is able. What is He able to do? He is able to do exceeding abundantly above all that we ask or think.

The word exceedingly is taken from the Greek word *huper*. *Huper* means high, above, and beyond. That is where the English word hyper is taken from. For those of us in medical sciences, we use hyper a lot: hypertension – high blood pressure, hyperglycemia – high blood sugar, hyperthermia – high body temperature. Hypo means low. God is able to do exceeding abundantly above, the New International Version says *'infinitely more'*, the Amplified Version says *'superabundantly more'*. God is able to do exceeding abundantly above all what we ask. The word for ask is taken from the Greek word *aiteō* which means to ask, to beg, to desire. The word translated as think is the

Greek word *noieō* which is to exercise your mind, to observe, to comprehend. So, God is able to do above all you can imagine.

I was telling my wife recently that my boys are very imaginative. I think they got it from me. My six-year-old son, Ethan, woke up early one morning, had his shower, and lay on the bed beside me and I was just watching him. He was looking at the roof. I just saw me in him. I said, *'Ethan you are thinking of something'* He said *'Yes'*. I then asked, 'What are you thinking about'? He said *'My comic character'*. I asked what the name of the comic character was and he said it doesn't have a name. *'Okay! What does it do'*? I further asked. He said, *'He converts shapes into cars'*. By the time I finished having my shower and came down for breakfast, he was drawing the character he was conceiving on the bed. My other son, Daniel, was in the shower and I just peeped because electricity bills have gone up and he goes to the shower for 30 minutes with hot water running. I went to peep at him and he was standing in a thinking position, hot water was running on his back. At his age, I was having my bath with buckets. He just stood there, hot water running, and steam was everywhere. When I was taking him to school, I asked him why he was just thinking like that,

'Do you have any problem'? I asked. He said, 'I was thinking of a ninja. I was just imagining myself as a Japanese ninja'. He started telling me about this ninja. So I told him that if he wants to think about Japanese ninjas, it should not be done in the shower as the power rate has increased.

But that is kids for you. They can be imaginative. They can dream, and they can create things because thoughts are limitless. Nobody can charge you any bill for thoughts. Imagination is limitless. Thoughts are boundless. You can think about an atom that you have not seen, you can think about Jupiter that you will never see. Nobody has seen all those planets, only pictures. You can think about Jesus and His apostles. You can think about the next Olympic Games. Thoughts are limitless but what you can ask is limited to what you need. So, imagine the limitless nature of thoughts. God is now saying that He is able to do above all you can imagine. I am trying to say to you that your imagination is limitless. Can my son become a Japanese ninja? He has no Japanese heritage but he can imagine himself as a Japanese ninja. God is saying He can deliver. What I am saying is that God can. So if my six-year-old son, Ethan, is thinking about developing a comic character that will turn shapes into cars, and he is already drawing and creating it, how much more will God not deliver in your life?

'Now to Him who is able to do exceedingly abundantly above all that we ask or think, according to the power that works in us' - Ephesians 3:20 NKJV

Power in the verse above is *'dunamis'*, it is the miraculous power. So, God's miraculous power is able to deliver according to the power that works in us. The word *'works'* is taken from the Greek word *energeō* which means to be operative, to be active, to be effective, to be efficient, to be adapted to accomplish a thing. So what it is saying is that God is able to do exceeding abundantly above all that you can think or ask according to the power of God that is in you, customised to fit into your story, customised to meet your need. Dunamis which is the power of God can be customised to produce results for you. The same power at work but the manifestation will be different. The same power, different manifestations, the same power, diverse gifting. So don't worry if your problem is getting a VISA. Some other people don't have VISA problems but if you hear about their problem, it is citizenship. Yours may be financial but if you know what someone else has under their stomach, you will take health more seriously than anything. You woke up today and you didn't have to take medication. Last night you went to bed and you didn't have to take a pill to sleep. I have heard somebody say, *'It is not money, I cannot sleep. I have not slept for 49 years without a pill'*. The power of God can be customised to meet your needs. So whether yours is a financial need, whether it is a spiritual need or a physical need, whatever it is that you need, today the same power and the glory of God will be customised to meet your own need according to the *dunamis* that worketh (energeō) in us.

If you are going to exceed expectations, you have got to connect with this scripture – Ephesians 3:20. Remember that your expectation is what connects you but if you are going to exceed expectations you are not going to rely on experience and instructions, you are going to rely on God Himself. You have to rely on Him. Abraham had an expectation for a son. In Genesis 11:1-7, we see the story of how God told Abraham to leave his father's house. Abraham walked out on his family to a land that God will show him. Abraham went with Lot. Lot was an entrepreneur. Even though Lot was under Abraham, Lot had his enterprise. We later find out that Lot had his staff. Lot didn't want to be in a combined family business. Lot had his people working for him, Abraham had his people working for him but both sets of workers were cooperating. The servants of Abraham and Lot were complaining that there was a problem – the land was too tight. So Abraham called Lot, and the two CEOs met. *'Our businesses are in a competition. So, let's solve it by expanding our horizon. Let's not fight over petty things. We are fighting over the same customers. Let's spread, we have land'*. Abraham explained. What do you think Lot would do? He should have deferred to his father figure, Abraham, to tell him what to do but rather Lot lifted his eyes and took the well-watered plains of Sodom. The best of lands. I am sure Abraham would have been disappointed about the person he raised as a son (because his father had died) doing something like that. The Bible says that Lot walked out of his life, he went to Sodom and Gomorrah. After Lot had left, God told Abraham, *'Look around you, on this land I will make your heritage like the stars'*. So when Lot walked out on Abraham, he lost more than a relative. Lot was the heir Abraham thought he had. He had no son and his wife, Sarah, was post-menopausal. Here was the person Abraham had set up but he walked away.

Let Lot go! Sometimes we put our expectations in Lot because we have invested a lot. Because Abraham had invested so much into Lot, he put a lot of expectations there not knowing that Lot was going to walk away. Everybody's journey is different, let Lot go! I used to worry before but I have stopped worrying now. That is just the nature of life, people have to move.

'Who against hope believed in hope, that he might become the father of many nations, according to that which was spoken, So shall thy seed be'.
Romans 4:18 KJV

Abraham hoped against hope. In Genesis 13, God already told him that he was going to be a father of many nations and in his own mind, he would have been thinking Lot was the person. You know the way we work things out. But against hope Abraham still hoped. That is the expectation that comes by revelation. Your expectation should not be based on experience or instruction. When your expectation is based on revelation, it will not be cut off. The people who don't give up on their dreams are people whose expectations are built on revelation. If your expectation is built on previous experience, it will be cut off. When it is challenged, you will find alternatives. If your expectations are based on other people's instructions – what they have experienced or seen and what they told you – it will be cut off! I knew when God was bringing me to this country and the things he had said he wanted for me. So, when everything was against me, when it looked like it wasn't going to happen, I went back to God, *'God you told me to come. You gave me that word, I believe in you'*. God delivered. When your expectation is based on revelation, it cannot be cut short.

So when we go back to where we started from – the finality of the statement that the expectation of the righteous will not be cut short – it is because the expectation of the righteous is based on the revelation of God's will. Nothing is as dangerous as a man who knows his purpose. He is ready to die for it. In the fight against terrorism, do you know why those 23 or 24-year-olds were willing to blow themselves up? It was because they found something. When you find something, when you know what God has called you for, it will come to pass.

The Bible talks about Isaac in Genesis 26:1-27. There was a famine in the land and God told Isaac not to go down to Egypt like his father. He was told to stay in the midst of the famine. God is telling someone reading this right now, *'Stay in the land'*! Stop looking for alternatives. You may be saying, *'God why did you lead me here'*? *'There is famine here'*! *'This business is hard'*! *'This marriage is difficult'*! *'You led me here, why am I in this tight place'*? and you start looking for alternatives and shortcuts. God said to Isaac, *'I know things are tight, I know about the inflation, but stay here'*. Maybe you are in your season of famine and you are trying to cut corners, you are looking for shortcuts, you are trying to leave, God says don't go down to Egypt. *'I know Egypt is bustling and prospering, stay where I have put you'*. Stay in the will of God. Stay like Isaac stayed.

'Then Isaac sowed in that land, and received in the same year a hundredfold: and the LORD blessed him'. Genesis 26:12 KJV

Isaac received in the same year a hundredfold harvest. There was a famine in the land but he sowed. He applied for the job, he registered the business, he sent applications, he talked to people, he did some marketing, he polished his CV, he changed his wardrobe, he shot his shot, and he sowed after instruction. Walk by revelation! In the same land where there was famine, where people were complaining that things are hard, he sowed and received a hundredfold. That is exceeding expectations. He exceeded expectations in the midst of famine because his expectation was based on revelation.

God is not a horrible God. He will lead you. He will show you and you will know it because there will be clarity in your mind. God will tell you what He has called you for. Don't walk away from that business, that career, that partner because of challenges. God's word to you is His backing and that's all that you need to not just overcome but to exceed expectations.

OTHER TITLES BY NIYI BORIRE

www.ingramcontent.com/pod-product-compliance
Lightning Source LLC
Chambersburg PA
CBHW031249290426
44109CB00012B/503